Love Around The M25

An Intrepid Dater's Quest For Love

By

Katja Leslie

Copyright © 2020 Katja Leslie

All rights reserved, including the right to reproduce this book, or portions thereof in any form. No part of this text may be reproduced, transmitted, downloaded, decompiled, reverse engineered, or stored, in any form or introduced into any information storage and retrieval system, in any form or by any means, whether electronic or mechanical without the express written permission of the author.

The views expressed in this work are solely those of the author and do not necessarily reflect the views of the publisher, and the publisher hereby disclaims any responsibility for them.

ISBN: 9798670115285

PublishNation
www.publishnation.co.uk

To all those brave souls who have opened their hearts and experienced hurt; who have dared to love and have lived from their hearts. To those who are keeping the doorway to love open with a smile. To all of you who are living this miraculous, messy, mysterious and monumental life with authenticity, curiosity and courage; this book is for you.

Acknowledgements

'Love Around The M25' is the result of my own personal relationship journey spanning approximately 11 years; some of which were tremendously challenging not only for myself but for my ever loving and supportive family.

Without the support of my family, through dark and desperate times as well as the lighter and laughter-filled moments, I would not have been able to grow into the person I am now, nor would this book have been written.

It is therefore with deep gratitude that I acknowledge and thank my family and the friends who have journeyed with me from the side-lines; to these people I give my heart-felt gratitude and respect.

A huge thank you to my friend and hairdresser Tracy for our wonderful conversations and her dedication to keeping any grey hair at bay! If it hadn't been for her encouragement in writing a book on my relationship journey, you probably wouldn't be reading this now!

I also thank those who have walked with me on this journey to the heart; the partners, dates and connections who have afforded me the possibility to grow, learn and mature as a person, and also as a therapist in my work.

Each connection is precious, no matter the outcome or experience; a nugget of gold along a journey of awareness and authenticity. For the dates that lasted an hour or the relationships that lasted much longer, I give sincere recognition and acknowledgement.

To my dear friend Hannah; whose bravery remains inspirational. Very much missed but loved always.

For my son, Scott, whose growth, wisdom and open heart continues to be the most precious gift I will ever experience, I thank you for our deep soul connection, your listening ear, ability to know exactly when chocolate is needed and rock solid support and clarity. You are an inspiration and it is an honour to walk this journey of life with you.

The names and some locations have been changed in order to respect the privacy of those involved in my story.

Contents:

* Introduction

* Your invitation aboard the good ship 'Relation-ship'

Chapter 1: The Mighty Pen

Chapter 2: Freedom

Chapter 3: The Meeting of Hope and the Camel

Chapter 4: You Give Me Chills

Chapter 5: Is That Really You?

Chapter 6: Depths of Diversity

Chapter 7: Who Said Romance Was Dead?

Chapter 8: Love Conquers All

Chapter 9: X Mark's the Spot

Chapter 10: The Gift

* Lessons Learned and Wisdom Gained

* Contact

Introduction

From a very young age I had an inkling that I had, just perhaps, chosen to embark on the unmade path of life, rather than taking the smoothly tarmacked one! Long before the days of sat nav's I found myself developing an inner compass and inherent pull towards and desire for, growth, knowledge and truth in all areas of life.

From a stable and loving family, blessed with a good education that fed my quest for knowledge and understanding, my childhood and adolescence were for the most part, calm and uncomplicated.

In my 20's I experienced a period of illness in the form of M.E. which steered me in the direction of self-help books and spirituality. I discovered a world, or multiverse should I say, that was expansive, exciting and ultimately freeing. A world that questioned my foundations of life and engendered an even greater thirst for true knowledge, far from the limitations of the education system that had trained me well to answer exams and fit into a mould of 'acceptability'.

Illness afforded an opening up of an entirely new perspective and set of questions and possibilities which were eagerly absorbed by a seeker such as myself.

Unable to work for a period of time, I read, researched and relished every book, workshop and connection to this fascinating expanse of knowledge that resonated at the very core of my being.

I began my training over 20 years ago in healing modalities such as Reiki and Energy Healing and subsequently became qualified as a Hypnotherapist, Psychotherapeutic Counsellor, Energy Healer and EFT practitioner. I also run Workshops and Meditation groups and feel privileged to connect with the brave and beautiful souls who I meet through my work.

Without the diverse 'story' that I am sharing with you in this book; albeit but one aspect of my life, I would not be the person I am now. And do you know what, after all these years of exploration, emotional upheaval, love, laugher and sadness, I have learnt to truly love who I am today.

It is my heart-felt desire to be authentic in all aspects of my life and work. This book is therefore my authentic, messy, tragic, humourous and wonderful journey which I hope will provide amusement, food for thought, opportunities for self-realisation and growth for each reader.

The path I walk along is still a 'work in progress' and at times I continue to navigate the potholes and road blocks that appear along it. However, it is with a joyful and peaceful heart and mind that I embrace the life I have journeyed thus far to create.

Your Invitation Aboard the Good Ship 'Relation-ship'

Let us embark on a journey onto the seas that carry us through singledom to relationship; *heartbreak, hope and unity*; together with the musings, meanderings and emotions invariably experienced along the way.

These days many find themselves single for a multitude of reasons such as bereavement, divorce, infidelity or growing apart, to name a few. Where previously couples were more likely to stay together 'until death do us part', relationships have evolved; some may say for the better and others for the worse, but whichever way you choose to look at it, the stigmas attached to being single or leaving a relationship have decreased. This change of societal perspective has, in itself, opened many up to seas of unchartered waters.

One view, historically held by society, is that there is something wrong with a single person; that they have 'failed' in some way and need to increase their endeavours to find someone to 'complete' them by being in a relationship and thereby deeming them 'socially acceptable'. It cannot be denied, therefore, that in spite of the changing tides, being single can for some, continue to engender feelings of failure, isolation and self-blame.

The pressure society often places on people to feel accepted can drive singletons to seek out a relationship; good or bad, simply to conform and be accepted; to tick boxes of acceptability and to no longer be the pitied recipient of the charitable dinner invitation amid a group of couples!

Let's pause for a moment and gaze out at the vast horizon before us as we find our sea-faring legs. Perhaps, just perhaps, being single is no longer a matter of lack of options, but rather, a choice oftentimes; a choice to *reframe* how you view your life; choosing to refuse to allow it's worth to be defined by your relationship status.

It is true that being single can be both liberating as well as terrifying; leaving the singleton navigating unchartered waters without so much as a life jacket!

In reality, reframing being single brings the potential to explore and enjoy being in a relationship with yourself. This relationship is undoubtedly the most intimate, precious and long lasting connection we will ever experience in our lives. In essence, the relationship with ourselves is the most natural one of all and yet it invariably appears as the polar opposite, with many finding it easier to be with others than with themselves.

It is healthy and customary to desire companionship and connection with others; we learn and grow through such interactions, be it family, love relationship or friends. Complications within the love relationship arise when the desire to be in a relationship is driven by the discomfort of being with yourself.

When we seek another to save us and complete us; filling in the loneliness and uncomfortable feelings, we invariably set ourselves up for greater heartache than is necessary. If we only sought to break through the conditioning and became happy and whole within ourselves before seeking love.

As you will discover through the meanderings of this book, I became a habitual dater; with the sole goal of finding 'the one', because the feelings and emotions, discomfort and societal pressure I experienced in being single were too painful to reside in.

Some leave the quest for love in the hands of fate or seek endless confirmation that he/she is on their way through psychic readings, while others turn dating site navigation into a full time job. I myself delved into each of these avenues; the search becoming something that I allowed to define me and at times almost destroy me.

In attempting to run away from being single I realised, over many years I hasten to add, that I was actually running away from myself; the irony being that there is one guarantee in life and that is the fact that I will spend every second of it *with* myself! There is no escape or running from me!

At some point I would have to realise this as the pertinent truth it is, work with it, accept it and nurture my most precious of relationships. It would be a journey of many lessons as you will discover; painful, poignant, powerful and at times, humorous too, but a most important and life-changing journey at that.

It involved a gradual peeling away of the proverbial onion to reveal layers of experience, growth and awareness. I had to cease identifying my worth and life with my relationship status and acknowledge that I am *not* my relationship and that my relationship status does not define me as a person.

Uncovering and discovering my self-worth was a huge part of the process in my journey towards self-love. Learning that my worth does not come from outside of me, through having a boyfriend or husband, was a powerful revelation and one that necessitated copious retakes of the exam, as my story will show!

I learnt to stay faithful to myself through focusing on self-respect; honouring my values, needs and standards, as well as creating boundaries within connections with others.

Love is our essence; it's at the core of who we are and yet we often don't invest the time in cultivating and nurturing our most precious relationship; seeking sustenance outside of ourselves in the form of romantic relationships. There can be no denying that such connections can be immensely powerful and precious; taking us to beautiful emotional highs as well as the deepest lows. There can be no doubt that the love relationship enriches our lives in a multitude of ways, affording tremendous growth and experience.

When we do embark on the good ship 'relation-ship' we can choose to bring with us the wealth of knowledge gained through working through our fears and previous experiences; knowing that once we set sail on this ship which invariably takes us through choppy waters and calm seas, the key is to learn to navigate them with full awareness. This ensures that we empower our relationships to make us wiser, kinder and more compassionate; creating deeper, more authentic and pleasurable connections.

For the ship to sail smoothly it is vital that we clear away some of the views or behaviours connected to the idea of relationships, which invariably do not serve conscious growth and authentic connection.

Focus has primarily been external; seeking to make ourselves whole and happy by getting something from outside of ourselves. This invariably brings disappointment, resentment and frustration as we are placing the barometer of our happiness on external factors.

When we find ourselves clinging to relationships out of emotional insecurity or eternally searching for a relationship which will provide us with the missing piece of ourselves we haven't found yet, we realise we have been placing our emotional wellbeing at the feet of another, rather than owning it for ourselves.

How often do we remain in a relationship because we feel we either can't do better or don't deserve better? I know I wore this particular t-shirt a few times! We so often allow ourselves to be around those who consciously or subconsciously seek to bring us down, diminish our essence or control us because we feel unworthy at core level.

Many people will choose to ignore or suppress the fact that people change and grow and as such, this means that we can't force a relationship to always remain static out of fear of change or need.

Over time, many of us realise that we cannot go backwards or hold onto old and perhaps familiar ways of viewing relationships; not if we want to live in authentic awareness. We have come to a point where fewer people are prepared to live lives of control or obligation, where fear or need is attached to relationships. As I discovered myself, it is frightening and challenging to set sail into unchartered waters but this has to happen once the call to authentic living and being has been spoken.

The journey forward involves awareness and appreciation that all positive personal progression starts inside; this is the fundamental key to creating the lives we desire. A powerful component of my growth was in recognising that our external relationships reflect our internal relationships with ourselves. I.e. my primary relationship is with *myself* and all others are mirrors of it.

They are, in part, reflections of how I view myself, my self-worth and the love and respect I have for myself. I became mindful of the fact that I was drawing to me that which I was radiating about myself through my perception, view, words and thoughts about myself. In essence I had to become the captain of my relation-ship rather than a mere passenger!

In time, as I began focusing on loving myself; attending to my own needs and emotions, it lead to receiving the love and appreciation I desired from others in my life; in both relationships and friendships. When we are committed to lovingly living and walking in our truth then we will attract those of a similar vibration, as like attracts like.

I learnt to be what I wanted a partner to be. As such, I made a list of the qualities I sought in a romantic partner and began developing them in myself. In seeking to become complete in yourself you will be more likely to find completion in a partner. In honouring and giving yourself the love you seek you will come to a new relationship as a more whole, aware, healed and happy person.

On my journey towards love it was imperative that I cleanse past relationships; learning to forgive the hurts of the past; be it with romantic or other relationships. Each of the challenges, if we allow them to, will teach us so much about ourselves, as well as our strengths and will guide us to know what we do and don't want from future relationships.

I learnt that at the end of the day, I am the only one who knows what is in my head and heart; what my needs, desires and wants are. It made sense therefore to nurture that relationship, take good care of myself and as such build a solid foundation within myself from which to create and maintain a loving, balanced relationship with another.

Ultimately in sharing the journey of my own self exploration, growth and maturity through the myriad of relationships and connections I experienced along the way, it is my sincere wish that each of us create a personal set of boundaries, mind-sets, awareness and tools to navigate life and love from a place of balance and authenticity.

I also invite you to allow a space for humour to imbue your life and its diverse relationships and connections. Without humour; the ability to laugh as well as learn through my romantic journeying I would not, I believe, have created as balanced and healthy a perspective on this expedition of the heart as I feel I have.

I discovered that boundaries were created and respected through open and honest communication; communication without fear, obligation, need or agenda. Through truthful and non-judgemental communication, I learnt to speak openly and honestly about my needs and feelings after many years of suppressing and not giving respect to them.

In recognising and acknowledging my own needs and appreciating the inevitable change and growth that is inherent within relationships, I released fear and control of outcome; thereby creating greater flow, expression and expansion, with possibilities rather than problems being the key ingredients and focus.

Ultimately though I realised, many years on from where my story will shortly begin, that love and respect for myself and my journey lies in choosing to be in a relationship because I *elect* to be rather than because I *fear* being alone.

So it is that it is now time for me to raise the anchor as I invite you to set sail with me on the good ship 'relation-ship'!

Chapter One – The Mighty Pen

"Put your hands up against the wall ma'am and spread your legs." My propensity for blushing in full effect, I complied with the female prison guard and adopted a pose reminiscent of many an American cop show. Deemed contraband free, I was ushered through to a Spartan waiting room, trying in vain to diminish growing nerves. Reminding myself that as an Aries adventurer, finding myself in a Florida maximum security prison about to meet the man I had fallen deeply in love with was nothing unusual and most certainly an experience worthy of my star sign!

Perhaps I ought to rewind slightly…..

Spiritual therapist with acknowledged rescuer tendencies, the Cygnus spiritual magazine ad several years prior, inviting non-judgemental people to correspond with those incarcerated in America, was an emotive pull I could not resist. Passionate about writing, injustice and human rights I was soon putting pen to paper; thus stepping onto a path that proved to be life-changing.

In all honesty I had never really given much thought to those behind bars in my own country, let alone thousands of miles away. A distant relative had spent a minuscule amount of time in an open prison, but other than that, prison wasn't something I had previously formed much of an opinion on.

Piqued by compassion and curiosity however, I felt as if my eyes had been deliberately drawn to the relatively innocuous advert surrounded by offers of psychic readings, birth charts and spiritual retreats.

A married mother of one, living a comfortable life in the Sussex countryside, my life was calm and for the most part happy. I had overcome M.E. which had seen me give up a job as a school secretary and was studying various healing modalities on my quest to become a therapist. My husband was a caring man who worked hard to provide for his family; we had married relatively young and he had supported me through my health issues as well as my desire to study in order to embark on a career as a healer and therapist.

Like all relationships, ours wasn't without its challenges and hurdles. Always incredibly in tune with my feelings and emotions; beacons that have lead the way for me, though good and not so good decisions and experiences, I had begun to feel a burgeoning disquiet over the years. Disconnect and lack of true communication, coupled with both of us living with the effects of my having M.E., followed by complicated pregnancy amid the usual difficulties and conundrums of marriage, I gradually fell out of love with the man who I had shared numerous years with, as did he with me. We both felt and experienced a distance between us and grew apart as life's journey began to take us on different paths of interest.

It is often the little nudges, quiet signals and heartfelt murmurings in life that we ignore; perhaps on a conscious level, perhaps in a haze of obliviousness as life moves forward; seeds of disquiet planted and nurtured unwittingly by lack of communication, as well as the hustle and bustle of life masking the unrest.

For a multitude of reasons I had time on my hands in relative abundance. As I grew stronger health-wise, a natural desire to open up to the world again ensued. My son had started nursery school and alongside my studies I had the time and space to explore my passion for the written word by answering the Cygnus ad for pen pals.

My first pen pal, Terry, was a man in his 60's incarcerated in Oklahoma. For several years myself and various other men and women from the U.K who had also answered the initial pen pal ad, sought to support a man who, to us, had been given the unfathomable sentence length of 200 years for a mixture of petty crimes, numerous prison escapes, refusal to be a 'model inmate' and being present during a prison riot. We fought tirelessly to engage with prison authorises regarding the blatant abuse of human, legal and constitutional rights inflicted on Terry. We raised money for lawyers; for my part that consisted of undertaking a 13 mile sponsored walk in the blazing heat of summer!

Between us, over the years, we formed a determined group, connected by a sincere desire to see the corruption within the Department of Corrections dealt with and rectified, not just for Terry's sake but, as we discovered, for the hundreds and thousands of inmates in similar situations, where lack of financial resource so often meant lack of fair due process in the courts.

The work myself and others were undertaking was rewarding, frustrating and enlightening. From my personal perspective, I began to question the often automatic judgement myself and many others would display towards the whole strata of society. I began writing to several other inmates in America. The more connections I made, the more stories of injustice and legal malpractice I encountered, the deeper my desire grew to play my part in being a voice to those who were silenced. Aries warrior had donned her armour and was engaged in a battle of monumental proportions!

Did my 'hobby' of writing to prisoners impact my life with my husband and son? Absolutely. I would be presenting an airbrushed version of my story were I to state otherwise. Hindsight is a wonderful view and perspective to possess, and when channelled correctly, I do believe it is something that affords us huge growth and knowledge as we journey through our lives. However, at the time, I was ensconced in a cause for justice that took up much of my free time.

The relationship between my husband and I had continued to disintegrate over the years, with both of us unhappy in our situation and this eventually lead to us splitting up. As we adjusted to our respective lives, I continued writing letters, connecting with other people from around the world who were also friends to those behind bars; some of whom remain friends to this day. My studies also progressed and I started work as a part time carer for a disabled lady as I adjusted to being a single mother.

Time moved on and hundreds of airmail stickers later, copious insight gained into the lives of those behind bars and a wealth of appreciation for the lessons of non-judgment such connections afforded me, I came across a pen pal ad for Joe. Logic told me that I didn't have the space for another pen pal; intuition begged to differ!

Brown hair with eyes to match, a fellow lover of the written word and spiritual seeker, my interest and eye was aroused. Did I forget to mention the man in uniform part…..well, we are after all on this human journey to experience everything this world has to offer and, from the days of watching 'An Officer and a Gentleman', the uniform thing has even given this short-sighted girl 20:20 vision! Ok, so a prison uniform was not quite on a par with Richard Gere's 'vision in white', but it was still a uniform….right?

They say love is blind and that we lose our ability to reason or apply logic. Perhaps there is also a huge dose of karma and growth potential that ought to factor into the mix of ingredients that create relationships that rock the very foundations of who we are; leaving a residue that fundamentally changes us.

Those connections that heart and destiny *has* to explore; shattering our hearts so that we may grow with deeper understanding and healing, are profound life experiences that the soul yearns for. In this case, cleverly disguised as a rather handsome man in uniform who quickly captivated my mind and heart!

Finding myself in the waiting room of a maximum security Florida prison was the conclusion of several years of writing and snatched phone calls. Phone calls which were abruptly halted by a robotic Department of Corrections voice warning that the time was up after 15 minutes. Here was I communicating with a man who had nothing but time on his hands.

Childhood abuse and neglect had, it seems, set Joe on a path of juvenile detention and then prison. Blessed, or cursed, with empathy in abundance, I could easily understand why someone faced with such early trauma and a need to fend for themselves, would have to steal to eat and survive. Such a journey rarely has positive repercussions and Joe was serving a ten year sentence for burglary when our paths crossed and fate decreed that my life was to become a roller coaster ride.

We've all seen the headlines 'woman weds death row inmate', 'woman leaves Surrey suburbs to join Maasai tribe' and perhaps read in disbelief that intelligent, educated people would choose to veer so far off the road of 'normality' and 'common sense'. Yet here was I; educated and from a loving, middle class background, therapist and spiritual seeker, creating my very own set of salacious story lines by falling in love with Joe!

Perhaps love really does have no boundaries; perhaps its energy is able to climb mountains, cross oceans and even scale razor wire fences. Countless books, blogs and conversations over coffee are devoted to the topic. Love that can take us on a ride to the greatest highs and deepest lows. Love coursing through our veins, directing our lives and opening unforeseen avenues. Love that is mysterious, uncompromising, powerful and all encompassing; physical, emotional and spiritual bodies engulfed within its majesty.

I have always enjoyed writing. There is an old-fashioned allure for me associated with letter writing; a poetic connection that transcends today's texting and swiping left or right; a depth and mystery when pen and paper unite. The removal of face to face connection, the writers are forced to communicate in a way that so often engenders deep conversation. Worlds, feelings and experiences are shared on a level that a date down the 'Crow and Gate' pub has never replicated; although I have some merry tales to tell about such escapades too!

As the prison visiting room became busier with wives, girlfriends, children and relatives, my nerves were tempered with a curiosity for the reasons and stories behind the razor wire fences; the love, heartache, shattered dreams and fragile hopes of those waiting with me to spend time with their loved one. Love transcends many boundaries and coupled with hope, it can give sustenance and courage even within the direst of circumstances.

Remembering Joe's instructions to grab a table as soon as possible and a bottle of 'Mountain Dew' from the vending machine, I had a minor mission to complete whilst the air conditioning brought relief to the mounting tension as I waited to see if Joe would pass the strict criteria required for each visit or whether I had traversed the Atlantic in vain….

Mission accomplished and said table claimed, I watched as a line of inmates akin to an army parade filed into the visitor's room. A sea of blue uniforms and shiny black boots, I remembered to breathe as I waited to finally meet Joe. Years of words on paper were about to manifest into physical connection. I say 'physical connection' but the strict 5 second rule for a kiss and hug was ever present in my awareness as fear of disobeying visitor procedures, resulting in termination of the visit, flashed into my mind.

He was real…..he was there…..those brown eyes, that smile and our first embrace; the harsh reality of our environment, situation and fantasy of a future together melted into insignificance as we took those first tentative steps together.

Given that many visitors had traversed state lines, driven for hours, or, as in my case, flown across the Atlantic, weekend visits lasted for six hours. However, six hours felt like six minutes; time having the ability to distort and disguise itself according to the situation. Holding hands across the table, we picked up where we had left off in our letters; laughed, joked and flirted. The seeming insanity of our connection, the apparent pointless pursuit of a life together and knowledge that such a union would require more hurdle jumping than an Olympic event felt insignificant on that hot Florida day.

It was a day of many 'firsts', ranging from first prison visit, first kiss and first use of a microwave! This holistic minded adventurer had not allowed a transatlantic journey, or nerves to defeat her, yet the prison microwave was almost a battle too much! Asking Joe, who was nine years into a ten year sentence for advice did not prove to be fruitful. Thankfully the more adept microwave frequenters steered me in the right direction and before I knew it I was merrily picking off pepperoni pieces to create a vegetarian pizza and enjoying an all American feast!

Goodbyes are never easy, but knowing you are relinquishing your loved one to a system where pepper spray, rape, punishment and violence are so often the norm, it was heart breaking to let go of Joe's hand and watch him, along with the other men, withdraw from the joy and openheartedness they had momentarily experienced as they sombrely formed an orderly line and were marched out of the visitor's room to endure strip searches and a return to life on the inside.

Stepping out into the humidity of mid-afternoon I was overwhelmed as adrenalin began to dissipate and emotional fatigue washed over me. Pride at having held it together during the visit and sadness at having to leave Joe where he was, was coupled with a heart bursting with love and happiness; my emotional roller-coaster ride in full swing.

My dearest friend Jane had accompanied me on my prison road trip and my gratitude for her presence was immense. As we drove back to our motel in the sleepy town of Carrabelle, mind and heart were filled with awe for the experience and journey love can so often take us on. Clutching a Polaroid picture of the two of us taken by an inmate designated 'photographer', it felt as if our journey had shifted from fiction to reality.

The following day, swimming in the clear blue sea, I saw two dolphins form a perfect arc in the sky as they leapt and played in the water; free and in unison. I wondered whether this was a sign from the universe that my story with Joe held the potential for union and was only just commencing. I had always read and believed that we are capable of creating our lives; that our thoughts and intentions manifest into reality and I started to believe that perhaps there really would be a future for myself and Joe.

It is also said 'be careful what you wish for'; little did I know that I was unleashing a powerful creative force as the wheels of conception began to weave, as yet, unseen, threads, interlacing Joe's life even more strongly with mine.

The remainder of that initial epic journey to Florida passed in a haze of sunshine, declarations of love on postcards to Joe and run ins with the local cops; an inevitable outcome of letting two British Thelma and Louise ladies loose on America's shores!

Thankfully Jane's penchant for nude sunbathing, yards away from a stern sign declaring that such behaviour would result in a fine, and illegal U-turns on a highway, did not result in she and I donning the not so attractive, in my eyes, female prison uniform!

Saved by our ever so polite British accents and feigning total ignorance, together with a smattering of liberally added apologies, we safely boarded our flight home to the U.K., memories in abundance, personal medals for bravery earned and microwave initiation completed!

Pen reacquainted with paper upon my return, Joe and I continued our Guinness Book of Records-worthy level of letter writing with increased fervour, love and connection. As the days and months passed, we grew ever closer to the date I had circled on my calendar – 2nd December 2006 - 'Release'.

Chapter Two – Freedom

School girl memories of the 100-m relay race enforced upon us each year came flooding back as I made a sprint to catch the connecting flight. Prison guards were no match for U.S. immigration officials and over several prior visits to America, I had perfected my subservient, non-Aries demeanour when seeking to gain entry to the 'land of the free'.

Several years supporting various human rights legal applications of those who had become friends behind bars had created confusion, as the 'liberty' and 'equality' elements at the nation's core had repeatedly been abused. My spiritual beliefs and learning had found me at odds with an absence of moral, ethical and humanitarian regard; resulting in laws blatantly being broken, human rights discarded and lives shattered by those supposedly 'correcting' the law breakers in prison. Little did I know that my spiritual beliefs would be tested in ways I could not imagine; corruption of power being only the very start!

Of course the intervening time was not as smooth and fast as my sprint to catch my connecting flight. While I had adjusted to life with my son; my parents living next door to us, the reality of loving someone in prison was far from romantic! Controlled, rushed phone calls, mail strikes and delays, a myriad of emotions ranging from hope to fear, happiness to anxiety, as well as saving money for flights and accommodation, meant that I became used to living with a foot in two worlds. Part of me was mother and therapist, the other was dealing with the highs and lows of loving an inmate.

Dealing with the emotional repercussions of disciplinary action against Joe, resulting in withdrawal of phone calls or mail privileges, would play havoc with my feelings of anxiety and dread; never knowing how long we would be without contact for, and more poignantly, having no way of ascertaining whether Joe was safe or not. Receiving a longed for letter which took two weeks to arrive would have me floating on cloud nine, whereas the same cloud would turn to thunder and rain when a hasty phone call from a fellow inmate informed me that he had been sent 'to the box' for two weeks for rule infraction; prison lingo for solitary confinement.

As you can imagine, adrenaline and I became, unwittingly, firm friends as I sought to live my life in England to the best of my ability, while my fragile heart was flipped more times than an all American pancake!

Sprinting to catch my flight, I made it with minutes to spare; adrenaline in overload; nerves intermingled with excitement and disbelief that I was making my final journey to prison; not for a visit, but to welcome Joe into the 'free-world'.

That evening we gathered together; a motley crew of 3 pen pals who had connected with Joe over his ten year sentence. Brought together; the most unlikely of friends who had a desire to welcome Joe into his new life, we laughed and joked and calmed nerves by enjoying drinks; listening to the crickets chattering equally loudly during a humid Carrabelle evening.

It is, of course, not a simple case of the inmate walking out of the gates as you see in the movies......For months prior to his release, Joe and I had exchanged zealous letters and phone calls arranging for his 'release' clothing to be delivered from the U.K. to the Florida prison. I do believe that engineering his escape may well have been easier! Having been trapped in a ten year time warp, I was understandably concerned that his clothing taste and request would have reflected this, but thankfully that was one fear that wasn't realised!

It was therefore on a hot and sunny December day that saw us waiting several hours for linen-suited Joe to take his first steps in over a decade into freedom.

He was thin, his head shaved and nervous as he took those tentative steps into my arms. For the first time in several years there was no threat of disciplinary action for flouting the 5 second hug and kiss rule! Freedom indeed! A kaleidoscope of emotions intermingled; jostling for position as Joe and I embraced. Not knowing until the minute he walked out a free man whether his release and behaviour would open that door....we'd done it!

In a convoy of two cars we made the drive to our hotel and base for the next few days. Stopping en-route for 'free-world' food, Joe's emotions ranged from apprehensive, excited to tearful and overwhelmed.

Arriving at the hotel, celebrations ensued; Joe's birthday the following day resulting in much merriment and champagne! Joe was an excitable child trying to take in sights, experiences, tastes and feelings that had been denied for a decade. Saying goodbye to his friends and having been kindly gifted a second hand car by one of them; we embarked on a road trip from Florida to Arkansas. It was here that Joe was to start his new life staying with one of his friends who had been part of his welcome party, while he waited for a passport and chance to fly to England.

They call it 'the honeymoon phase' don't they; a haze of connection and emotion that belies clear vision. I was truly embracing the 'now' and honouring the gift the present moment is; in a whirlwind of adventure as we traversed Alabama and Mississippi; in love, in lust; enthralled with this man who had called to me from the unconscious yearnings of the soul. A connection that logic and sense could not prevent. A fated and powerful union. We laughed, cried, loved and planned for our next chapter together.

Were there any thorns present on the rose stems or was I truly wearing those tinted glasses with abandon, I ask myself? In the early days I felt as if I had connected with the embodiment of all we read about in soul mate books; resonance, union against the odds, intellectual, physical and emotional stimulation, coupled with spiritual vision. A Hollywood movie made real and Joe and I were the stars!

The small gifts that appeared 'out of nowhere'; 'gifted' I soon learnt from unsuspecting shops. The wandering eye which I naively equated to the 'kid in a candy store' analogy that any person would reasonably have after being deprived of the opposite sex for so long. These thoughts began to creep into my peripheral vision. However, in this hub of blissful discovery, union and Hollywood-worthy script, these minor details were but dimly chiming melodies; very far from the alarm bells they would subsequently become!

After a week in a cabin in the beautiful Arkansas forest, my two week stay was drawing to a close and the reality of being separated once more reared its head. Indeed, reality in all its guises was upon us as we faced the uncertainty of waiting to see if Joe would be granted his first ever passport; the first of many hurdles we would need to overcome if we were to realise our dream of him moving permanently to England. Job, money and dealing with a long distance relationship where prison bars no longer denied us union were all now a reality, but laws and visas were now our adversaries.

A tearful goodbye at the airport and I once again let go of the man I loved; holding the vision of permanent union in my heart as I flew back to England.

Joe mastered the alien technology of Skype, got to grips with a mobile phone and snatched conversations broke up the weeks of uncertainty and waiting. "I got my passport" he declared! A three month return ticket was hastily arranged and before we knew it, Joe was on his flight to England.

Aside from a moment of panic when customs phoned me while I was waiting at Gatwick, to verify that I was Joe's partner, the 3 month tourist visa was granted; no side-stepping of the law, but a genuine window for Joe to visit the U.K. while we embarked on the rather more complex task of applying for a fiancé visa.

The initial weeks together were for the most part happy and harmonious, as Joe underwent a vast culture shock and adjustment to middle class life; life as a step-parent of sorts as well as living with me full time. Looking back I see that I was on a high; in a bubble and haze of joy and sheer amazement that he was now actually living in my home; something we had previously only dared to dream about.

Joe, I realised was also on his own high, but this, I discovered to my shock, was the high of being more than someone who 'smokes the odd joint to relax'; rather, a full time weed addict. His deft assurances that he was in the process of giving marijuana up and that he was merely continuing so as to ease himself into his new life, gave me hope and I, with my ever present rose-tinted glasses and Hollywood 'happily ever after' vision, believed and trusted that his words were sincere.

Naivety and hope; a staunch belief that it would naturally take time for Joe to adjust were coupled with times of sincere happiness together; fun and carefree moments which, in spite of the signs, provided me with the misguided belief that our love would conquer all and that time to adjust was all that was required.

Even then, the barely audible whisperings of my intuition; drowned out by the rescuer I was, as well as quite possibly my ego not wanting to entertain for a second that perhaps I had misjudged the situation myself and my family now found ourselves in, were clamouring to be heard. Joe had the charisma and intelligence that enabled him to talk, cry, utter sincere desires to change and grow into a better person and in my nativity I believed him. I wanted to believe him because the alternative was to admit or even begin to acknowledge that just as Little Red Riding Hood had allowed the wolf into her home, so too had I, unwittingly, unleashed my own 'fairy tale' into existence.

"It's like a wild animal has been released" my father declared after Joe had been living with us for a month. He was not wrong. There was by this time no denying that Joe struggled to adjust to living outside of prison. Perhaps I ought to elaborate. I am aware that the passage of time and many years healing wounds on a deep level has also undeniably eased the memories of emotional and mental pain my family and I endured.

Joe came into our family like a tornado; uprooting every foundation we held dear. At the time my son and I lived next door to my parents; one property split into two and so it was that I will forever bear the awareness that my choices deeply impacted those I love the most. We learn through our choices, mistakes and the forks in the road we take. Joe has, on a deeper, spiritual level, taught me more than any counselling or therapy course could ever have given me. The resonance I hold to this day of awareness of the impact domestic violence has on a family is something I have learnt to channel for the good; supporting those who come to me with their own versions of my story.

I also hold deep understanding for why, many of us who are thrown into the maelstrom of emotional conflict when the person who professes to love them, proceeds to cause untold pain and devastation, do not end the relationship forthwith. Hope is the last to die and I, like so many men and women in similar situations, held hope in my heart until the last vestiges of it were shattered and I reclaimed the power I had allowed Joe to hold over us.

While those on the exterior of such 'stories' see the simplicity that ending the abusive relationship ought to be, it is an entirely different story experienced by those within its pages; love interwoven with fear, hope mixed with hopelessness, happiness tainted by sadness and logic linked to lunacy.

He cheated. Well…I never had 'concrete proof', but there were enough signs, hastily closed down websites and emails, from someone who was naïve to internet navigation and thereby left himself open to being discovered. The friendship with my dearest friend Jane broke down for a number of years amid allegations of Joe cheating with one of her younger relatives. Joe's moods became erratic and angry; my home being reduced to smashed furniture and crockery on various occasions.

He lied. He stole from my boss and then he bought flowers and cried and sought counselling and swore to change and become a better man. And hope, the eternal hope within me kept burning. We attended couples' counselling, but within half an hour the session turned into a one woman band as Joe stormed out of the session; angry, defensive and tearful at being faced with his actions by the counsellor. And so the pendulum swung from hope to despair and from despair to hope as time moved on and Joe's visa came to an end.

As such he returned to America after the three months had passed; our fiancé visa application process necessitating that he apply from his homeland. We had instructed a Human Right's lawyer to support our application for fiancé visa and had been informed that we stood a fair chance that it would be granted. Over a year passed and I visited Joe twice during this time.

Although I can look back over this period of my journey with awareness of the threads of the tapestry I was weaving and the growth it afforded, at the time I struggled between the whisperings, and sometimes full blown screaming matches, my soul would declare. My soul would urge me to let go; release the flames of hope and assimilate that love doesn't mean hurt and that it is often not destined to last in terms of our human relationships.

Standing at the check in desk at Heathrow for my second post prison trip to see Joe in America, I felt crippled with indecision as to whether to board the plane or simply go home. I was not immune to my intuition and the impact the situation was having on my health and the wellbeing of my family......but hope.....continued.

My second trip to America was one of turmoil. Joe had been asked to leave the home of friends he was staying with amid rumours that he was spending his time surrounded by the very people he had been involved with prior to his ten year prison sentence; drug dealers, prostitutes and petty criminals. It was, as such, a shock to me to arrive at Dulles Airport in Washington to discover that we were in fact going to be staying in the local Holiday Inn rather than with his friends; a kind family I had spent time with on my previous trip.

There had been a plethora of rumours both during Joe's three month visit to England as well as during his time back in America, yet I remained loyal to the hope and vision I had fought so hard to manifest. Typing these words many years on, I find it unfathomable that I am that same person. I don't say this from a judgemental or harsh stance but from the perspective of who I am now with the wealth of knowledge and growth life has since afforded me. However, it still astounds me how we have the capacity to live such very different stories within one lifetime; exploring the many different journeys, experiences and realities that this human voyage affords us.

So it was that January 2008 saw me spend the new year with the man I still loved dearly; a man whose heart I believed to be true, but whose outer persona had been deeply marked and affected by his life choices and experiences. The ability to see the good in everyone is not, as I discovered, a badge to be worn with pride; rather, in my case most certainly, and undoubtedly fellow rescuers will perhaps also echo my sentiments, a sign of deep sensitivity that requires careful protection, understanding and awareness.

The challenge is, as I have discovered in the wonderful realm of hindsight, to present the rescuer with a mirror so that he/she has the opportunity to acknowledge and assimilate their own needs, values and reasons for charging ahead with, in my case, blinkered vision on their quest to rescue another!

Let's not forget the Aries warrior either; recipe for rescuer tendencies in abundance!

Chapter Three – The Meeting of Hope and the Camel

Hope had quite a quest in front of her, but ever ready for a challenge she donned her finest battle regalia and rode off in search of her rainbow!

Hope floundered as Joe's fiancé visa was denied and my reserves on both a physical and mental health level were deeply affected. Adrenaline is an interesting thing, for it so often, by its nature, sustains you through challenging situations only to cause emotional, physical and mental crashes afterwards. I was barely aware of the impact the judicial process was having on me because living on adrenaline, with insomnia and anxiety thrown into the mix had become my 'normal' state.

The reality of living on a knife edge; with doubts about Joe's behaviour and integrity rife, as well as being a mother and focusing on working, was very far from the rose-tinted outlook I had viewed our story and situation with from its infancy. I turned to psychics in a desperate attempt to receive some optimism about our situation. My spiritual practice became askew as it developed into a plea-bargaining contest between me and my spirit guides; give Joe and I a proper chance to see if we can work together and I'll meditate every day....I'd promise the earth if it meant, in my desperation, that Joe and I could be together.

Hope was reignited as I sat, with my mother, in the Court of Appeals in London. My lawyer gave a compelling speech as to why Joe should be afforded the chance to prove his positive transformation by coming to England to marry the woman he loved. The book I had been prompted by my intuition to write some years prior; which ironically had been published in

America, proved to be a major component in swaying the judge's decision as Joe had contributed to some of the chapters with me. Our visa denial, as such was overturned and Joe was allowed to travel back to the UK on a two year visa, under the condition that we marry within three months of him returning to England.

Our wedding day was a happy occasion. I felt as if life had given us the 'ok' to finally create some much needed stability in our relationship. The initial months were filled with calm as Joe relaxed into knowing that he was finally 'home', could apply for a job and begin his life anew. In spite of his obvious need to work through and release the conditioning of his past, Joe was desperate to find employment and contribute to the family and he secured a job with our local supermarket with ease, worked hard and began to make friends. Life seemed, at least for a short while, to settle into an easier routine.

There was however, no denying that Joe's transition into a more sedate and calm life was ever going to be easy or straight forward. He seemed to create chaos wherever he went; partly through utter nativity and lack of awareness of how to live outside of the prison regimen, as well as not having to beg, steal or borrow in order to survive. Our patterning swiftly becomes ingrained within us and Joe's former lifestyle was challenging for him to overcome.

There was also a side to him that wanted to be able to combine both lifestyles, but this is impossible due to the opposing realities each presents with. He both railed against and desperately sought 'normality' and the security of a family after never having received this as a child. It was as if two conflicting forces were interplaying within his mind and heart, creating a pendulum that swung between tears and terror within him as well as for myself. It was as if he didn't possess the skills and awareness that most of us take for granted having been raised by loving parents, supported through education and early life. Indeed this lack of guidance, support and love in Joe's early life was undoubtedly a key component in forming his misaligned personality, morals and coping abilities.

I have always loved driving and a telling indication of where my head and heart were transpired when Joe crashed my beloved Ford Focus, swiftly followed by my replacement Renault Clio only a few weeks later. I was more upset at seeing my crushed cars than Joe being led away in an Ambulance.

Surely hope had hitchhiked out of my life by this time, I hear you ask? Alas hope hung on for another year longer. A holiday was what Joe and I needed we decided. We had never had a honeymoon so we saved and decided to take a week's holiday to Corfu. It was during this holiday that the severity of Joe's marijuana addiction became abundantly clear to me.

He was a master of hiding his activity at home and, not wishing to police his every action; knowing that distrust was deeply unhealthy for a relationship, I had decided to trust his words when he would go out with friends or be away from home. Perhaps now I can reframe those actions of mine as having been deeply naïve as well as having been driven by a desire to hope for and see the best in Joe. That, as well as sweeping certain behaviours of his well and truly under the proverbial rug! The rug, as you can imagine, became overladen with hidden behaviours, emotions, realisations and feelings, but it wasn't quite ready to head to the dry cleaners!

Corfu; an island of sunshine, romance, simple, easy living and a chance for us to connect, converse and chill out; not so in our case….. Without his contacts to enable his weed addiction, Joe faced a week of being without his crutch and support system as he saw it. As such, rather than seeing it as an opportunity to face his demons, he turned to alcohol as a means to cope with his longing for drugs.

He became morose, aggressive and his behaviour erratic and at times, frightening. The holiday was in fact so dire that I considered purchasing a separate flight and returning to the UK alone, leaving Joe in Corfu. The anxiety that I had, for the most part, managed to keep at bay, awoke with a vengeance during our holiday and I experienced panic attacks for the first time in my life.

Joe's behaviour was both shocking and embarrassing; he appeared to have no qualms about causing a scene in the hotel restaurant or on a bus trip to Corfu Town, rendering me tearful as well as fearful. I was never fearful for my safety in terms of physical reprisals; rather it was the relentless emotional abuse that Joe, sadly, so often resorted to, especially without the weed to mask his demons, which affected me severely.

I knew and have always known that I am a strong, independent person, but here I was shaking and subservient; doing my utmost to appease a man for the sake of peace, who had confused my head and heart with his mixed signals; professing love one moment and displaying hatred the next.

Upon our return I had made my decision to face the reality that my marriage had to end; however Joe promptly sought out the support of a counsellor, began regular sessions and did his upmost to reduce his marijuana consumption. And hope……..hope reignited; albeit for less than a year more. I do believe that part of Joe genuinely wanted to work through his issues and craved love, stability and acceptance. However, it had become very apparent to me that his demons were too strong for even love to conquer.

Throughout my journey with Joe, I had sincerely believed that love would triumph over all and that Joe simply needed more time to adjust after the abuse of childhood and prison; time, something he had had on his hands in abundance in prison was something that ran out for us in June of 2011.

The straw that breaks the camel's back is, by the nature of the expression, invariably a minor incident and indeed, this it was. Joe had chosen to spend a weekend, where my son and family were away, with friends rather than working on our relationship and seeing if we could move forward. Connecting quietly inwards I was finally in a space to hear the whisperings of heart and mind. It wasn't a momentous lightning bolt for me; it was a split second knowing that that was enough.

The light of hope, which had been burning so brightly for several years, was extinguished in a moment and I knew, finally, that I had to summon all my reserves of energy to end my marriage and remove Joe from mine and my family's lives.

Empathic, naïve, rescuer and spiritually minded person I may have been, but once heart and soul knew that enough was enough there was no turning back. So it was that I took a deep breath and told Joe the marriage was over and within days his bags were packed and our break up commenced.

Part of my fear, and perhaps hesitance, in ending my marriage sooner was due to the fact that I knew Joe had no family or friends in England he could turn to or stay with. I felt on some level, responsible for his wellbeing; having been the one to bring him to the U.K. Misaligned responsibility of course, but none the less, I felt, from a compassionate standpoint, that nobody deserved to be made homeless.

A turbulent few weeks ensued whereby the police were involved as Joe tried to break into our house, refusing to accept that the relationship was over. His mental state became increasingly fragile and erratic. My ever decent family ensured that he had a roof over his head so that he had the opportunity to get on his feet and so that we may be spared further attempts by Joe to come to the house.

In late August of 2011 my son, mother and I spent a week on a pre-arranged holiday to Cornwall. Neither my mother, nor myself were in holiday mood as you can imagine, but for the sake of my son and the realisation that being in Cornwall would provide us with respite from the ever present potential for Joe to return to our home, we set off.

I had contacted a psychic I had had readings from previously and arranged for her to give me a telephone reading. It so happened that she could only schedule a reading for the time we were in Cornwall. Familiar with readings and a believer in all things spiritual, I presumed it would probably be what had, by this stage in my turbulent relationship with Joe, a familiar run of the mill reading. My loved ones on the other side would tell me to end my marriage and, I hoped, inform me that all would be well now that I had finally done so.

There followed the most disturbing reading I have ever experienced. The psychic told me in no uncertain terms that a man I had recently split from posed a significant threat to myself and my son. She provided details and information she would have had no access to other than from those 'upstairs' as I like to refer to departed loved ones and spirit guides. As I sat at the kitchen table in a lodge in Cornwall I was told that this man was not prepared to let me or my son leave his life so easily and that he had the very real potential to kidnap my son so as to hurt me in the worst way possible....

What do you do when you receive such information? Already vulnerable and scared, the reading compounded the fear that was already very real and present within the mind of myself and my parents. The psychic had recorded the reading and upon emailing it to my father at home he immediately phoned me to say that, while his was sceptical in many ways of such readings, he was so convinced by the detail and urgency with which the information was given to me by the psychic, that it would be safest if my son and I could leave our home for a short while until the potential threat had decreased. Liaison with the police who had been incredibly supportive confirmed that such a move, while not compulsory, would most certainly be a sensible step to take given the circumstances.

I had been told in the same reading that a friend's partner with an Irish connection would help me to find an empty house to rent. As I wracked my brains in an attempt to ascertain who this friend might be, one of my closest friends contacted me to see how our holiday was going. As such it transpired that her partner, of Irish descent no less, had just placed his house at the coast on the market, having recently moved in with her. He offered his house on a rental basis for as long as we needed it.

The following week saw us travel from Cornwall to our home and from our home to Eastbourne where my son and I and two of our cats set up home for a couple of months. The move necessitated temporarily taking my son out of school and we found a friendly home education group to join. Brisk walks by the sea, connection with friends who came to visit us and my studies as a Hypnotherapist, filled our time as we lived in a bizarre limbo life as my divorce proceedings continued; my having filed for divorce the very day the camel's back broke.

Wide awake one morning at 4 am, hope was reignited by an inner passion to reclaim my power from Joe and to move back to my home without fear. The final hurdle hope needed was to face Joe in order to show myself and perhaps him that he had no power over us and that I was indeed well on the way to the next chapter of my life.

So it was that our lives returned to a semblance of normality and other than a few attempts to contact me or reignite our relationship, Joe left us alone, eventually moving on himself with his own journey.

We are survivors by nature and my family and I slowly began to release the traumas of recent years. Regardless of the outcome, Joe was an integral part of my journey and I do not believe regret and guilt serve anyone. Rather, I sought to commence the long journey of releasing guilt and regret, and to commit to learning the tough lessons presented to me as opportunities for growth, for service to good and to remembering the intrinsic essence of why we incarnate on earth and why we adopt these human vessels with our complex stories. Mine as you can tell by now, was not quite worthy of a Disney star on the walk of fame!

Five months later this journeying soul decided to dip her toe for the first time into the world of online spiritual dating and soon found herself almost freezing to death; perhaps a slight exaggeration I will concede! However the temperature did require hats and coats, mittens and bed socks to be worn in the home of her subsequent Devon suitor.

Chapter Four – You Give Me Chills

The months after my split from Joe and return to our home in Sussex were spent creating a quiet and peaceful space for my son and I to live in and a search for 'normality' where life had been anything but for too long. I continued my work as a carer as well as my studies to become a Counsellor and Hypnotherapist.

In spite of my belief that guilt is a burden that serves no one, I admit that I carried considerable responsibility and regret within me which needed to be worked through as part of my healing process. It was incredibly important to me that I ensured that those whose lives had been affected by my decision to bring Joe into the country knew without a shadow of a doubt that I was deeply sorry. Sorry for my naivety, rescuer-driven desire to create a happy unit with Joe and the ensuing pain and trauma it had caused my son and parents predominantly.

The past had happened; there was nothing I could do to change the script or outcome but there was plenty I could do to ensure that I learnt, grew, soul-searched and demonstrated through behaviour, word and action, that I genuinely had gone through a steep learning curve in my personal post mortem of the relationship with Joe.

I made a promise to myself that never again would heart, head or attraction blind me to the love of those who truly mattered in my life; my family. Never again would my son have to experience the trauma of decisions I took; albeit from a heart-centred and somewhat naïve perspective, with no awareness of the maelstrom connecting with Joe would create.

As life regained its balance, I realised that for the first time in my adult life I was truly single; a new phenomenon for me and something I set out to explore in more depth! It was a curious situation to be in because it was such an alien one. School, university and work had created a near constant relationship status which meant that considering stepping out into the world of singledom was a new and somewhat daunting prospect.

I noticed I became obsessed with spotting whether people were wearing wedding rings and would allow such symbols of a couple's union to bring waves of sadness and fear to me. As the summer suntan covered the white mark of the band I had worn when married to Joe, I realised that if I was to hope to trust men again and not allow the past to dictate the future, I would have to take a deep breath, conjure up some bravery and launch myself onto the world of online dating.

The spiritual dating site seemed to me to be a more gentle toe-dipping way of exploring the terrain of online dating and so it was that I created, somewhat tentatively, a dating profile. I was a little dismayed to learn that there were very few 'matches' within even a 60 mile radius of my home. I was even more dismayed, upon venturing to the profiles of those suggested to be a match, to discover to my horror, that pickings were truly limited and very thin on the ground....not to mention wholly unattractive to my initial untrained dating eye!

My joy at receiving my first ever message was short-lived as upon reading the content I realised that my 'match' was suggesting I join his harem, for want of a better word. Very little deliberation was required as the message was relegated to 'junk'.

I pondered what type of 'spiritual' connection I was looking for. What 'spiritual union' represented to me as well as to the other souls exploring the same site and ethos? Spirituality, as I knew from my own journeying into the realms of the metaphysical, is a vast, infinite exploration with many interpretations, beliefs and directions. I'd never previously been called on to overly clarify in my head and heart as to what constituted a positive relationship because I had effortlessly strolled from one relationship to another.

My two previous marriages had been polar opposites in every way and neither had lasted. While I fully subscribe to the belief that two people unite in order to learn and grow through the union, and that longevity of relationship is not necessarily a marker of 'success', I needed to delve into my own heart in order to ascertain what it was that I was in search of.

My 'list' comprised humour, respect, friendship, attraction, intelligent conversation and a genuine desire to grow and learn together. I had read copious books on the law of attraction and on manifesting your soul mate; I was all set, surely?

Enter Justin from stage left…..

"Your voice and our connection feels like a ray of sunshine from Sussex to Devon" Justin enthused during one of our early conversations. With beautiful blue eyes and a mop of dark curly hair; he exuded a peaceful, nature-loving energy; just what the doctor ordered after events a few months previously! Having studied in Devon, the south west has always held beautiful memories for me, so I was happy when the spiritual dating site declared Justin and I to be a match. I was also happy that there seemed to be no harem joining or polygamy in the mix!

I was surprised to connect with someone so quickly and relatively easily and wondered if the universe was rewarding my bravery at 'getting out there' by bringing me a potential boyfriend so soon.

Talking of doctors, mine had been very supportive through some very dark days during and after my split from Joe. She informed me that it was not for most people to open their heart again after what I had endured and that my determination was a positive trait that would see me through traversing the road to love.

It is not in my nature to give up; that Aries optimism and fire never extinguishing even when reduced to embers at times. What could be the harm in slowly exploring the dating scene; nothing at all, except that slow and steady were not terms I was overly familiar with!

"Come over for Christmas!" I declared a few weeks into speaking with Justin. "If nothing more, we know we get on well as friends, so come and join us!" And so it was, Christmas Eve of 2011 that Justin made the 5 hour journey in his battered little blue car and appeared once evening had arrived, windswept and hair running amok under his hat.

It would be rude not to crack open the wine on Christmas Eve and we did just that; easing into a fun, easy going evening with mild flirtation and myriad diverse conversations. I wasn't totally sure whether relationship potential was on the menu and so it was that early Christmas morning saw us stagger somewhat merrily into our respective beds; Justin ensconced in the spare room while I navigated a burgeoning hangover in mine!

The Christmas period passed in a whirlwind of feasting and long country walks; sparking the connection of fledgling romance. Taking me for a meal out on his final night, Justin asked whether I would like to visit him in Devon in the new year. Devon, sea air, beautiful countryside and cosy nights in his cottage; what was there to say no to?

I spent many a childhood holiday skiing and even have the photo evidence of a grumpy four year old, in putrid green ski flares I might add, freezing in her skiing class with cold fingers and toes and the kind of cold exhalation of breath that is akin to puffing out a cloud of cigarette smoke! So, fire signs and cold are not natural companions, but I was hardy and adventurous and a cosy log fire beckoned, surely?

Reminiscent of the grumpy four year old, I was blasted into an ice cave without the vodka and ambiance to compliment the chill. Justin's 'cosy' cottage had, he proudly informed me when I arrived one January afternoon, never experienced the central heating his landlord had, sanely in my view, installed.

There wasn't even a drop of wine, nothing to take the edge off the kind of cold that chills you to the bones. Justin however, busied himself chopping wood and contentedly lighting his log burner; wisely decked out in beanie hat and 'sensible' clothing. The ensuing cosy fire and the momentary defrosting of limbs gave me hope that I could weather this frosty reception. Ah hope, my friend, ally and that glass half full part of me that, at times, I simply wanted to drain every last drop out of and declare myself teetotal from!

Showering became purely functional and undressing was not, as I had anticipated, something associated with allure and romance as I spent the subsequent few days with Justin. Any notions of passion and naked abandon were quashed amid a need to conserve body heat! Trips to nearby sights, beautiful coastlines and an area steeped in history also became precious opportunities to bask in the car's heating.

Justin, as you may well be gathering by now, was an interesting fellow. He embraced the concept of living at one with nature and being in tune with the seasons. He exuded a peaceful, school boy charm which, in spite of his reticence to align with modern facilities, afforded him an aura of calm and tranquillity, which didn't render him entirely unattractive. Perhaps, after the hot-headed maelstrom that Joe had been, Justin's presence in my life was to connect me back to simplicity, quiet and nature.

Or possibly, experiencing the polar opposite of Joe, *arctic in fact*, in this peaceful countryman, provided an opportunity to realise that perhaps balance does not need to scale mountains and grip tightly onto roller-coaster rides in order for it to be experienced. Perhaps, balance is inherently discovered within.

However, waving goodbye and gleefully flinging my winter hat onto the passenger seat as I gave my trusty Peugeot the opportunity to show me its full heating capacity, this particular spiritual seeker knew that she learnt through experience and that this chapter was not yet complete.

I began to realise that I had an affliction or ability to see the best in everyone; obviously this trait had been in full effect during my relationship with Joe; seeing the heart essence of someone who behaved in the very definition of all that was not love. I had not, at this point, learnt that love does not mean hurt and that hurt is not a requirement of the journey to a successful relationship.

I had yet to assimilate that many turn to relationships to experience security and comfort; for safe harbour. Yet all too often a paradoxical thing happens; the relationship itself becomes a cause and source of fear, upset or turmoil. These were mere whisperings on the periphery of my spiritual awareness and growth at this stage of my relationship journey. I had yet to fully assimilate that I could experience a fearless, mutually respectful relationship based upon true compassion.

I also had much to learn and understand about self-love and self-worth, for they, at this stage, were merely terms I was familiar with. I had most certainly not integrated their meaning on a deep, inner level and was simply paying lip service to their integral importance; not only in understanding myself but in clarifying what it was I deserved, wanted and felt comfortable with in terms of a relationship with someone.

I continued my short-lived relationship with Justin and was a thoroughbred at long distance relationships by this time; Devon being a brief stroll down the road in comparison to Florida!

Upon his next visit to my home he related positively with my son; something that was, as you can imagine, a vital ingredient in the mix of my relationship requirements. Bonding over wood work and gardening, it warmed my heart to see the two of them connecting.

Justin was a calm and balanced person, spiritually aware; something that I enjoyed conversing with him about. He was a very self-contained person however, an admirable enough trait, except that I began to sense that he would be reluctant to relinquish his Devon abode or share it with others if the relationship ever became more serious.

Looking back I realise that his presence in my life was partly to assist me in moving on from Joe; an opportunity to disengage from the storms of recent years and to begin to reacquaint myself with Katja.

My final visit to Devon saw me loading not one but two heaters into my car; content with my plan to bring warmth and comfort into my impending sojourn with Justin. Navigating the country lanes to his somewhat 18th Century abode, I felt excited and positive about the following days. Reaching his home as evening fell, I was tired and hungry, but felt bolstered by the knowledge that I would soon be seeing Justin again.

Did my ears deceive me or did he really find the appearance of the two heaters both amusing and insulting? A fellow Aries, there was no holding back from Justin as he informed me that there were to be no heaters in his home; declaring that his log fire would suffice and that frugality with bills was paramount.

I didn't have the energy or desire to challenge his affront at the presence of the heaters the evening of my arrival, so I tapped into the inner ability I had perfected during my relationship with Joe, of withdrawing into my own counsel, energy and space; a tool that has served me well throughout my life. As they say in the sunnier climes of Spain, 'Manana'; I would tackle this latest challenge in the morning.

Manana, however, came sooner than expected, with both of us sitting by Justin's fire as flames turned to embers in the early hours and conversation turned to 'us'. Fellow Aries will recognise that our sign is one of bravery, honesty and openness; admirable traits, except when it meant being faced with stark truths and no window dressing of emotions!

"I don't want to be with someone who has a child," Justin declared. "I'm not ready for a serious relationship and think we need to split up." Noah's flood had nothing on the water works Justin's words provoked. Every drop of sadness, pain, loss and trauma from my relationship with Joe, which were buried very close to the surface, seemed to flow out in those early hours with Justin.

While I was fully aware that my reaction was triggered by the unhealed recent trauma with Joe, it dawned on me that Justin's heart held similarities with the temperature of his cottage; his reactions cold, measured and almost disinterested. His naivety in expecting me to see out the remainder of my planned stay 'as friends' was concerning, as was the fact that he appeared more upset by my refusal to do so than our split.

After a few broken hours sleep I bid a tearful farewell to Justin and began the journey home with my trusty heaters in the boot, counting the hours until I could be reunited with my family and the central heating!

The ensuring weeks were filled with tears and T.L.C. I realised that I had perhaps been slightly naïve in expecting or hoping for love to fall into my lap so easily. Looking back I was seeking to fill the hurt and pain of my experiences with Joe through external love and security; assuming that the remedy was to be loved by someone else.

While I can retrace the steps in the years following my split from Joe and view the subsequent connections made, with self-awareness and deep understanding regarding the gift each held on the road to self-love, I still had many miles to travel in order to reach that particular destination.

We can read, study, YouTube and discuss love and relationships all we want, but ultimately one has to reach the clarity, peace and happiness that only truly dawns when we *become* within ourselves that which we had previously sought externally.

And this particular book would indeed be very svelte if I knew in 2012 what I know now!

It was time to expand my understanding, awareness and experience of this still relatively alien and complex world of dating sites; to cast my net further afield and join more mainstream sites than the seemingly safe world of spiritual dating sites.

Millions do it; it can't be that challenging to navigate, surely?

Chapter Five – Is That Really You?

Rarely lost for words, I found myself with a severe case of writer's block when it came to penning the all-important profile information. Scanning my companions on the dating site I could make out the 'pouting princesses', 'high maintenance madams', 'grounded goddesses' and 'nervous novices'. Some poured life stories and traumas onto the site, while others cautiously exposed the bare minimum of information; hoping to circumnavigate this online terrain.

It dawned on me very quickly that the dynamics of online dating were more complex than navigating the M25 in rush hour. Too much information and I was at risk of seeming overly desperate, too little and I could be perceived as aloof or harbouring dark secrets.

One click and my profile was live; casting my line into the sea of hope, lust, dreams, dramas and, it soon dawned on me, men with a desire to expose themselves in more blatant ways than by the written word! I soon realised that for some men, the appropriate introduction was to seek to obtain your phone number as soon as possible; not to speak or converse via phone but so that they could introduce their private parts as, one can only presume, a 'hello' to entirely replace the need for a written message or phone call!

I have never been drawn to fishing, but one thing I soon learnt was that, while the sea may appear abundant with offerings, like the pearl in the elusive oyster shell, patience, perseverance and a dose of realism were very much on the menu for this novice dater. Discerning truth from fiction and reality from fantasy were skills even dear Monsieur Poirot himself may have struggled with in the land of online dating!

Furthermore, recognising the dates at the designated pub or café was something that even the sharpest of eyesight would have encountered difficulties with. I struggled with the notion that having a profile picture that was ten years old would somehow entice the date once they met with the unairbrushed, older version.

Who doesn't dream of being swept off their feet by a tango enthusiast? Local, with the potential for some fancy moves, my online conversation with Rob was lively and fun. Meeting one Sunday lunchtime at my local pub filled me with joyful expectation. It is said that expectation is an unhealthy pressure to place on another; one which will inevitably only lead to disappointment. And indeed it did. My initial dating dalliances were consumed with naivety; whereby I sincerely thought that each would be 'the one'; that we would connect instantly and the rest, as they say, would be history.

I soon learnt that my gut feeling and instinct in those initial moments of first meeting someone were the precious signals sent to me in order to save me from having to dig deep into my growing repertoire of escape plans, excuses and 'emergency calls' from family. Suppressing a yawn I told myself that, with an interest in psychology, I could reframe my date with Rob into one of psychological exploration once I realised that no amount of fancy foot work could entice me onto his dancefloor!

From Fagin's boy to Hiawatha, I had perfected my drama skills from a young age and while Broadway hadn't been my destiny, I had the perfect opportunity to master the art of acting. Failing that I soon realised that steering the conversation onto the more spiritual topics of my therapeutic collection would invariably stun my date into dazed silence. After all, surely it was perfectly normal to discuss the merits of various past life regression techniques and my 16th century life as a monk on a first date?!

The size of the loo windows people escape from when faced with a coma-inducing date in the movies are vastly exaggerated, I discovered. 'Emergency text' from my mother however was carried off to perfection and thus mine and Rob's tango wasn't to be.

Perhaps fossils and history were more appropriate? Arriving at Battle station to meet with Andrew, I spotted a tall, dark haired man who thankfully resembled his profile picture. Fossil hunter by day and poet by night, I was intrigued to learn more about my date as we settled down for afternoon tea in a quaint café.

Being a lover of mysticism, signs and symbols, I soon began to ponder whether the universe was eavesdropping on our somewhat stilted conversation as scones and tea were delivered to our table. Could the initially appetising looking scone with a slightly stale and hard interior be a message to tell me to arm myself with Indiana Jones style excavation equipment and escape to safety before boredom-inducing mummification ensued?

Having studied Archaeology for a year as part of my university course I adore all things archaic and historical; uncovering intricate stories and legends of times gone by. Yet the prospect of enduring another hour of fossil dialogue, coupled with being 'serenaded' by relic- infused poetry was creating more brain freeze than embalming!

Being invited back to Andrew's bedsit to inspect supposed fossils was a proposition too far and as such I bid adieu to shattered fantasies of moonlit beach walks with dulcet, dreamy poems being whispered in the moonlight. Rather, stale, stilted and laborious conversation would see me hurling myself into the waves!

Back to the dating drawing board I realised that personality, panache and positivity were qualities I needed to explore when sorting through potential suitors.

In phone conversations, Rich from Essex was dynamic, witty and gentlemanly enough to drive to my local pub for our date. Flamboyant stories of army adventures and business blunders made for light-hearted and enjoyable repartee as I found myself warming to this quirky fellow.

However, happiness turned to hopelessness as Rich took it upon himself to order whisky upon whisky by the double, knowing full well that 'mi casa' most certainly was not going to be 'su casa' post-date at the pub!

Rich's slurred sexual advances and salacious suggestions saw another layer of dating disillusionment descend upon me. As Rich's 'charm' turned to chunder I made my way home, leaving him to experience an uncomfortable night in his car as he texted apologies intermittently during the night, subsequently increasing the number of blocked numbers on my phone!

Dalliances with dating sites was rapidly becoming a full time job requiring MI5 level skill set, vigilance and vast amounts of humour and patience. Having had long term boyfriends since discovering boys at the mixed school my parents transferred me to at 16, I was faced with the stark reality that, while there appeared to be an abundance of single men allegedly looking for love on dating sites, in truth, it was a minefield of disillusionment, disappointment, discernment and discovery!

For many, myself included, dating sites can become an unhealthy addiction, fuelled by loneliness, disappointment and the 'success stories' that adorn the home pages of each site. I became convinced that if I put more time into the search for 'the one' I would speed up the process and would ensure that I didn't miss him, as scrolling through profiles became an obsessive pastime. Similar to the 'just one more chocolate biscuit' scenario, I would sneak another look at profiles after I had told myself today's search was over; just one more......and another.

It's only in retrospect, as I pen these words, that a wealth of learning and awareness has afforded me a healthier perspective. I wasn't ready to internalise the knowledge that seeking something to the point of obsession; feeling lonely and incomplete without 'the one' and placing my focus externally; giving the power and potential of my happiness outwardly rather than creating it from within me, was only going to align me with the very signal I was emitting. Hence I was emitting a strong signal of neediness, loneliness and incompleteness and my experiences were mirroring my state of mind at that time.

Today I look back at my experiences with the fondness of a mother looking at her child grow up as they experience the trials and tribulations, highs and lows of discovering life. I see threads of absolute perfection in all of the situations, from harsh to humorous, because they have given me such self-awareness, empathy and growth, which have benefited my work and personal life immeasurably.

So, with the seeds of growing awareness not overtly apparent, I was perusing the dating sites with a determination and vigour that surely saw me standing on the podium with the gold medal! I had, by this time, joined several dating sites. There were those that professed to have the technology to match people perfectly. I delved into those that required hours of input of vast amounts of personal information and those that could be joined in an instant. The results from one site manifested in marriage offers and dates from far flung continents; the site having clearly no regard for the measly parameters it asked prospective members to put in place when completing the online application to join.

I soon realised that online dating sites were also a hotbed for scammers; the suave army captain with impeccable credentials, financial abundance and perfect pearly white teeth who was in fact part of a scamming ring operating out of Nigeria. Thankfully I didn't fall prey to such blatant exploitation of those who were vulnerable and sincerely looking for love, but several of my friends did.

One was serenaded by bouquets of flowers that would arrive and it wasn't until she was asked to wire money to enable her zealous suiter to obtain the necessary paperwork to enter the U.K. that she realised that both she and her dreams of true love were nothing more than a con artist's smorgasbord of pickings. Another friend sent her life savings to the man who professed to love her. As such it soon became apparent that there was indeed a darker side to dating sites and that, as with many aspects of this human journey, there are those who seek to profit from the vulnerability of others.

My dating journey continued, thankfully armed with a little more awareness and discernment.

One evening I met the atheist who was determined to convert me from angels and ascension to anonymity and dust. Alas even several drinks on it became obvious that I was a lost cause in steadfastly remaining loyal to the angelic realm rather than relinquishing them for obscurity!

Unfortunately my non-believing date seemed prepared to surrender his beliefs in return for a second date and thankfully through a slight alcohol-induced haze I was able to convince him that I was in fact more likely to become an atheist than see him again. As such, I was, albeit slowly, learning that the complex dating scene required a dater to often times be cruel to be kind and that there was no place for false hope or slurred agreements to meet again if heart and mind were screaming a resounding 'no!'

Shortly after my 40th birthday I met Marco the Italian vegetarian chef who tantalised my taste buds with delicacies and an accent I thought I could dine out on forever. Several dates ensued after our initial meeting at a beautiful vegetarian restaurant in Brighton and I held high hopes that this meeting would prove more fruitful than the fated evening with the atheist some weeks prior.

Hesitant as I produced my vegetarian lasagne to a vegetarian chef, I was amazed and slightly enamoured when Marco enthused over my cooking skills. I was fairly certain that it wasn't his lack of English that prompted such delight; perhaps I really had hit the dating jackpot after all?

Although there had been none of the Italian romance one so often dreams about, I must admit to being slightly saddened upon hearing that Marco had lost his job as a chef and had decided to move back to his family home near Rome. I had hoped that this slow burning flame would perhaps grow into something quite special, but in spite of declarations from both of us to remain in touch, this vegetarian pairing was simply not to be, as distance and time extinguished the fledgling flames of connection.

A brief date with a film buff who munched more enthusiastically on his popcorn and love for film than he did with conversation and connection, ended before the closing credits appeared. As such I returned, somewhat battle weary, to the dating drawing board.

There was the recovering alcoholic who was still in love with his ex and the music enthusiast who saw being denied a date as an opportunity to seek me out in my local Morrison's in the frozen fish aisle to proclaim undying love. A date with a suitor from Wimbledon appeared to flow with sublime spiritual synergy until the second date was cancelled due to his spirit guides informing him in no uncertain terms that the timing wasn't right and that we were not to meet again!

Apparently, some months later, a snake animal totem declared to him that we were indeed destined to be together and he contacted me for that elusive second date. Thankfully, a longstanding snake phobia brought me to my senses and a swift 'no' text was sent.

A new plan was formulated on my quest to finding love as the realisation dawned that shared interests would prove to be the key that unlocked the elusive prize of love.

Sebastian was a Canadian yoga instructor from the Isle of Wight and we seemed to have an initial connection albeit via the medium of email and sporadic phone conversations. It was agreed that he would make the trip from the Isle of Wight to Brighton and that I would meet him there for our date.

Strike one occurred pretty instantly as Sebastian got into my car and saw my yoga mat sitting pristinely on the back seat. There was I thinking that this would engender an immediate connection and symbol of shared passion for yoga. Such visions were swiftly shattered as he told me that many people kept their yoga mats in their cars; meaning that they only saw the inside of a yoga studio once a week for their prearranged class, rather than the more diehard yogis whose mats took up near permanent residency in their homes for their daily practice!

Alas strikes two and three occurred shortly thereafter as it became apparent that our taste in music varied enormously, as did his desire for connection with someone who would want children; something I had clearly stated as being non-negotiable on my dating profile! As such the yogi from the Isle of Wight boarded his train home as I made the drive home to mine, no closer to finding my other half.

The stories, situations, smiles and surreal experiences continued into the early summer of 2012 when a house move saw me focus on more practical aspects of my life. Before entering the momentary enforced withdrawal of Wi-Fi moving house would create, I happened across the longest, funniest, most open and heart-warming profile I had seen along my search thus far.

A theatrical story book of life, with its refreshingly honest words, I hastily bookmarked Dan's profile page. I was intrigued and excited to potentially connect with him once I had moved house and found the computer from the multitude of boxes that I would have to wade through. Very soon I hoped to make contact with the man from the coast whose smile and eyes captivated me and whose words had me crying with laughter.

Chapter Six – Depths of Diversity.

House move complete and Wi-Fi connected, I was able to pursue the initial communication Dan and I had initiated previously.

Several video calls had me in stitches as he regaled stories old and new of his colourful life; dating dalliances and disasters, crooning as he played his guitar, smoking cigarettes and drinking red wine all the while. I had forgotten to tick the box that would have prevented smokers from contacting me, but was secretly glad I hadn't remembered because Dan presented as a loveable rogue; affable, theatrical and rather nice on the eye too.

I heard him before he even arrived at my front door. Being serenaded by a flamenco dancing guitarist brought a momentary halt to the usually busy and bustling main road I had just moved to!

Dan appeared with full concert passion; energy, enthusiasm and raucous laugh to match as I ushered him into my house; hoping the net curtain brigade opposite had been otherwise engaged and as such spared the performance, as well as my shock.

His laugh and smile filled the house with a lightness and vibrancy that was engaging and addictive as we chatted openly and easily like two old friends reacquainted. Within hours of meeting I knew of Dan's millionaire status several years prior, the subsequent gambling and exotic holidays that saw him virtually penniless. He was open about his financial reliance on his brother who had chosen a different route with his inheritance; thereby providing stability and income for the two who lived by the sea with their dog.

Dan had a mischievous glint in his eye, a genuine smile and an engagement with life that was hugely endearing and a delight to be around. His stories were a plethora of adventures from the risqué to the ridiculous, the sublime to the salacious and I found myself warming to this charming chap who brought laughter and life back into my world.

Our first date lasted from mid-morning until the evening as we laughed and talked, shared stories and snippets from our respective lives.

In my eyes; as you have no doubt already discerned, wealth, status, background or beliefs were no barrier to my open heart. While I have, without question, learnt and grown from the myriad connections with the men I met, and created a level of awareness and maturity regarding matters of the heart, for me it has always been important and indeed vital to meet people from a space of authenticity rather than superficial judgement.

Naturally the rose-tinted glasses I wore with abandon in the early years of my dating dalliances were relegated to a dusty box in the attic, but it was always important for me to view each person in an expansive rather than constricted manner.

I can reminisce over my experiences with fondness and a fervent desire to always be lovingly responsible for decisions made and lessons learnt; choosing never to become bitter or cynical about life's journeys; seeing them constantly as threads of the aforementioned tapestry; creating a unique record of diversely interlinked colours and fabrics.

Rescuer tendencies? Most certainly!

From my first interaction with Joe, I had empathy in abundance and was most likely wearing a siren and florescent high viz jacket in the eyes of the men I connected with. I provided a safe haven and open heart; playing the role of rescuer to perfection and ignoring my own needs and fragile heart. I was focusing solely on the misguided belief that to be loved I had to give of myself, heart and soul to another even if it was to my detriment.

Was I ready to acknowledge this salient information in 2012......what do you reckon?!

I'd heard of O.C.D and Bipolar in my therapeutic training but had never connected with someone bravely facing, at times, seemingly insurmountable mental health issues. Dan had been transparent with me from the outset; explaining in detail the rainbow of emotions he could experience in any given day.

His honesty laid bare the demons he faced and engendered a respect from me that created a stronger connection between the two of us. I felt, for the first time in years, safe and heard as I shared my own journey with anxiety and insomnia; borne out of many years of stress, especially from the experience with Joe, with him.

My honesty over my relationship with a former prisoner shocked Dan and initially he withdrew from our tentative relationship as he was fearful that Joe could still pose a threat to me and as such, to him. I understood that he needed to ensure that his mental health was as stable as possible and I also had to learn that while my 'story' with Joe was simply my 'story' or part of it, to outsiders it could be quite a shocking and unusual tale to hear. I was relieved however when Dan agreed to continue our fledgling romance.

During our relationship which spanned just over a year and a half, my son and I spent many an enjoyable weekend with Dan and his brother in their home. We grew to love walks by the sea with his dog and it was as if the easy laughter and genuine connections enabled old hurts to be released that little bit more. The sea, simplicity and laughter healed the past and soothed the soul.

Dan and I holidayed in France and as such he conquered long held fears of flying and travel. We seemed to overcome challenges; both with an awareness of the other's fragilities and emotional needs. We danced as we cooked pizza in his kitchen, drinking rose late into the night as we debated and delighted in our diverse conversations. My faithful feline friends grew to love his dog as did my son and I, and as such our relationship was a haven of happiness in many respects.

In the words of a favourite country music song, 'Time marches on…..' and so it was that talk between Dan and I would invariably turn to our living arrangements and a potential future. We existed in a delightful bubble of laughter and lightness for the majority of our relationship, but part of my being began to acknowledge that Dan disliked talk of commitment or altering our present living situations. Awareness of his financial position, coupled with the array of often conflicting emotions he would experience due to his mental health, he began to become frustrated when the topic of developing our relationship into a more committed situation arose.

I considered relocating to the coast to be closer to Dan, but as communication about the future became more tumultuous, I began, over time, to hear the same call of my being to step back and assess the situation. While the free spirit part of me was content to live the months and possibly years in a free flowing scenario, my heart began once more to whisper and tell a story of stability; urging me to listen to the burgeoning disquiet that was echoing within me.

Towards the end of our relationship I discovered that I was pregnant in spite of being on the pill at the time. I knew that our relationship was not stable enough and nor had I intended to have another child and, as such, I underwent a termination. Dan supported me to the best of his ability, although the stress and procedure I experienced caused his mental health issues to exacerbate. Our relationship further deteriorated, through neither of our intentions or faults. Rather, it was due to the combination of personal, financial and geographical situations we found ourselves in at the time.

In the movies the love struck couple rush to meet each other half way along the path of life; with compromise and consideration affording the possibility of lasting union, but in our situation I began to feel that I was a solo traveller in this particular movie clip, with the threat of thunder in the distance.

As such, communication disintegrated into confusion and animosity and I made the difficult decision to end the relationship with Dan. Heartbreak once more became a familiar companion as I began the journey of disentanglement of heart and hope from another. My love for Dan had been genuine and my heart was heavy in the ensuing months after our split.

However, the legacy of the relationship with Dan was one of truly happy, carefree and fun times together for the most part. My role now was to make peace with the fact that relationships are invariably complex things which require an intricate dance of connection, compatibility, camaraderie and care; none of which necessarily guaranteeing a life-long rapport, as I was realising more and more over the years.

Heartache saw the acquisition of two kittens; cementing my badge of honour as 'Crazy Cat Lady' as I added to my family of unconditionally loving cats. The coast, once a source of joy and happiness became an endurance test in those early months as I confronted the pain and loss of my relationship. As the autumn turned to winter and hibernation of heart brought the necessary restoration, I once more aligned with the hope and glass half full attitude which is my inherent nature and began to live my life again.

As my glass filled and heart healed, the pull to engage with the male species once more increased and I found myself again typing my all-important dating profile into a couple of sites, as the promise of 'finding the one' emblazoned on the home page lured me in and relit the beacon of hope within me.

Was the universe prompting me like a reticent school girl, to assimilate and move to the next grade in learning the self-love and worth lesson once and for all? As the ever faithful dating sites matched me with two suitors I departed on my next set of adventures; not at the same time I hasten to add!

Pete passed the 'showing the photo to friends' test with flying colours; unbeknown to him of course and as such, phone calls turned to meeting and plans became reality. On a scale of dating experiences; bearing in mind mine thus far had invariably ranged from the disastrous to disbelieving and downright dire, my date with Pete was a huge success! Conversation flowed, flirtatious glances were exchanged and smiles were abundant as we wended our way around the pretty market town we had chosen for our initial rendezvous. He ticked the proverbial dating boxes and as such a second date was arranged.

Several dates turned into the first flurries of a relationship as Pete and I grew closer. He was, unlike some of my experiences, someone who kept in regular contact via text or call and seemed kind and considerate. Add in a dash of attraction and it appeared the ingredients of a blossoming connection were in the mix. The etiquette for texting is varied isn't it and I think we invariably find a level, or at least seek to, with the person we are with; one that seems balanced and natural for both.

It soon became apparent that perhaps Pete's scales were misaligned as his texts become torrents and calls copious. My much loved swimming or yoga sessions became sources of angst and anger for Pete as he was without reply to his messages during this time. Evenings of peace and tranquillity became Spanish Inquisition scale interrogations about my movements. It became obvious that Pete's emotional responses were neither healthy nor balanced; his need to know my whereabouts at any given moment of the day or night were obsessive and also highly unattractive.

Discussions aimed at discovering if a middle ground could be attained proved fruitless as Pete's possessiveness continued and the inevitable conversation to call time on this particular connection ensued. Subsequent weeks saw gifts arrive, guilt projected and suicide threatened. Far from being unfamiliar with the pain that emotional loss can provoke, I attempted to provide an empathic and balanced ear to Pete's conversations.

Eventually he sought the help he needed to deal with unhealed grief from his prior divorce and the calls and contact abated. Many years on Pete continues to email once a year, usually on New Year's Day, to attempt to re-establish contact or perhaps resurrect a relationship. Self-worth however, shared her wisdom with me and as such the emails remain unanswered.

Self-worth, it appeared, had work still to be done though and the required grade to master this particular life lesson had not yet been reached. Ever diligent at school, I was; subconsciously of course, keen to assimilate the required knowledge and understanding in order to excel in this subject!

Enter Stuart; socially unaware, shorter in real life than his profile had suggested and somewhat boring to boot. I would not blame you for wondering why I entertained such a situation; indeed I am speechless as I reminisce. My only defence would be that miss rescuer raced to the forefront of my awareness; desperate for recognition and resurgence. Stuart's motorcycle accident had by the account he gave, been an horrific one and the sight of this man hobbling towards me on our first date; together with the abundant compliments he showered me with, was enough to draw this particular adventure out in a most unnecessary fashion!

Initial relief at Stuart's reticence to maintain contact after Pete's polar opposite behaviour, turned to confusion as days or weeks would pass by without contact. Stuart was married to his job as a scientist and I quickly became relieved that I would not be the one to break up this happy union.

Boredom and a distinct lack of common ground within the few dates we shared, coupled with several brief visits to each other's homes, transitioned into the inevitable relief once I decided it was time to bid Stuart adieu. The M25 which had by this time become both friend and foe, depending on the date or destination, was most certainly relegated to foe on the few occasions I journeyed to Stuart's home; the stress-inducing journey of an hour and a half doing little to engender me to this already flagging connection!

And so it was that minimal conversation due to my disinterest in all things scientific and Stuart's reticence to discuss the spiritual, together with a distinct lack of attraction once the rescuer had abated, surmised that it would be a mutual 'no brainer' to end this particular dalliance forthwith.

However, Stuart's parting words of "but I love you and want you to move in with me" shocked and surprised even this seasoned dater!

Chapter Seven - Who Said Romance is Dead?

As you can probably surmise, the written word is a delicious aphrodisiac to me and as such it was intellectually stimulating to connect with Thomas online. A fellow writer by day, Thomas was a photographer by night; a delightful and intriguing mixture which ticked important boxes in my ever growing list of requirements.

Thomas was handsome too, and as our messages increased in both length and fervour I found myself looking forward to my daily intellectual dose of connection with the rather amiable man from Kingston.

As heart and mind began the exciting prospect of yet another jaunt on what had by now become my local road; namely the M25, Thomas announced to me that, while we clicked on many levels, the geographical distance between us was too great to consider a relationship. Men and distance had been something I had encountered on several occasions over the years, resulting in many a road block on my quest for love.

It seemed that although the internet had removed barriers to previously impossible encounters, a milometer was installed in the heads of some of the men I encountered, rendering it 'no entry' to any distance that was deemed excessive. For some 'excessive' was 10 miles, for others 40 miles; each with their reasons, such as job, family situation or potential for that quickie 'popping over for a cuppa' mid-week date!

Hence Thomas and I became enthusiastic email pals across miles in 2014; rapidly forming a close friendship, acting as dating guru for the other as we both continued with our respective and ever increasingly elusive search for 'the one'.

I decided I too could master the closer to home distance requirement and altered my dating profile accordingly; narrowing the field of potentiality as I typed in my 10 mile radius of acceptance.

There ensued the man pictured riding a camel whose messages contained very little other than innuendo without the intrigue and the Frenchman who was abundantly open in his profile, informing all who read it that his wife was completely on-board with his dating liaisons. There followed messages from a local policeman who, it appeared, was collecting salient, sensational and sexual stories from those he interacted with, in order to write his own novel perhaps. Needless to say I didn't take him up on his offer to attend a 'members only' exclusive car key swapping club in London!

Where was romance? Where was the art of dating and decorum? Having abandoned my distance requirement, I found myself once more in despair of there ever being even a hint of wining and dining, roses and romance... until that is Victor's profile announced the 'new member' status that all die-hard online daters craved; seeking to snap up fresh meat before they were caught elsewhere!

His profile picture set against the backdrop of Venice was accompanied by those elusive words promising romance and passion. Surely the plethora of drunken, dull and calamitous dates experienced in their masses thus far meant that I was more than overdue for love and romance? Did I mention Victor was another Italian?! Perhaps after the all too short connection with Marco, here was my second chance at romance with someone from the country of love. Smouldering looks. Passion.

Copious boxes ticked, message sent, I allowed myself to drift into haze of dreaming about fine Italian dining, hand in hand moonlit walks in Venice and red roses.

Our first date was in the distinctly non-romantic setting of Crawley! I found myself enjoying a very pleasant evening with yet another M25 connection who lived in Sutton. Sublime accent and impeccable manners, intelligent and worldly, I found myself quickly warming to Victor as we got to know each other over the coming weeks.

Dining out on pizza in an Italian restaurant one night, he reached his hand across the table and asked if I would like to fly out and join him in Italy where he would be spending some time in his home town over the summer? "Si si – bella idea." Romance was indeed alive and well and it appeared, sitting opposite me inviting me on holiday!

A whirlwind few days in Italy ensued and Victor and I grew closer. Upon our return there was even talk of moving closer to each other if the relationship flourished. Things did indeed appear to be blossoming.

After initial hesitance, Victor introduced me to his young son and, with our two boys, we experienced a couple of fun outings together. I would make the journey to Sutton mid-week to spend a night with Victor once he had returned home from where he worked in London and we enjoyed cooking Italian meals together and sharing snapshots of our respective lives.

I could tell however that Victor was holding back emotionally, although it could well have been more a case that he was emotionally somewhat immature or repressed. Perhaps, as had been my behaviour in previous relationships, I was too easily able to see beyond a person's exterior and view them without the baggage and wounding's that life invariably presents each of us with.

Looking back at the six months I spent with Victor I wonder if the notion of romance with the man who spoke the 'language of love' was more fiction and fantasy than fact. The time span between texts would increase from a day to four days at times, where Victor had initially filled my phone with "I don't want this to end; what we are sharing is something special". He began pulling away, spending more time with work colleagues and weekends playing football with the boys.

Far from a needy person, I took this in my stride, but seeds of disquiet seemed to have set in for us both. There wasn't an awful lot holding us together, fuelled even more so by his emotional reticence to share any feelings with me.

I noticed that weekends spent together consisted of us both catching up on his cleaning or chores the working week and his social whirl had denied. Passionate evenings became a chance for him to watch yet another episode of "24" on his iPad in bed; transferring romance firmly into relegation! In fact it wasn't just love making that became somewhat robotic and functional, Victor's interaction with my life, hopes and dreams diminished and as such I began to lose interest in the Italian who displayed none of the perceived 'stallion' elements we perhaps naively dream of when the movies and romance novels take us to Venice or Milan!

Christmas came and went and a trip with our sons to Winter Wonderland followed as December 2014 drew to a close. We talked of New Year's Eve plans and I was disappointed when Victor sent me a text message saying he had a cold and would be spending New Year at home.

I awoke on January 1st 2015 to the start of a brand new year and a text from Victor informing me that the relationship was over and that he felt he could never love again after the collapse of his marriage a few years previously. Telling me I deserved better and goodbye, I started the New Year with any romantic notions having firmly vanished, as well as consuming several bars of chocolate brought to me by my ever wonderful son, who knew that chocolate could fix many a broken heart!

Due to run a spiritual workshop a few days later, and having been there for Thomas through a particularly painful breakup a few months prior, he in turn was my support as I assimilated the end of another relationship. We had never actually met until Thomas asked if I had space on my workshop. Not having previously been into all things spiritual he declared that it was time he explored new avenues and as such would like to attend, which also gave us an opportunity to meet face to face for the first time too.

A final message in response to Victor's suggested to him that he may wish to seek to work on self-love and healing before embarking on any subsequent relationships. Sermon delivered I was ready to embrace my ever faithful source of love, balance and sanity, my spiritual workshop, aptly titled 'Creating abundance in your life'.

It was time to let go of the reins on the quest for love and focus on my work; teaching and coaching being a passion which had never faded. Indeed, as the human journey of love and relationships grew more complex and confusing, my beliefs brought an increasingly balanced outlook on the topic; much needed wisdom amid the chaos of courting!

Thomas was just as handsome in person as his photos had suggested and it took every ounce of professionalism on my part to ensure that the afternoon's workshop did not disintegrate into lower vibrational thoughts and visions! Professionalism scored a hat trick and the afternoon was a success. Post workshop, Thomas and I chatted about our distinctly dismal love lives and commiserated over the seemingly endless tales of rejection, confusion and misfortune both our experiences of dating seemed to mirror.

We discussed at length over the ensuing weeks, how, two aware, intelligent and not unattractive people could create such trails of emotional devastation and confusion in their dating liaisons. I cited karma as a distinct possibility whereas Thomas, more scientifically minded, felt it was a matter of human psychology, bad luck and lack of emotional awareness in most people. I didn't disagree; in fact, our conversations became engrossing explorations of humanity as we sought to discover the reasons why some people met 'the one' seemingly easily and why others, such as ourselves, appeared to be creating our own versions of Groundhog Day, caught in an endless loop of love, loss and longing.

As the weeks passed, I realised that I was falling for Thomas. Friendship gave me trust in him as a person; something which dating often denies or circumnavigates as flirtation and emotions open up different avenues. We were communicating and spending time together as friends and this had allowed a deeper bond to be created. My attraction towards Thomas crept up on me and then in a less subtle manner, slapped me in the face, rendering it almost impossible for me to be in his vicinity.

In one of our regular phone conversations I took a deep breath and informed Thomas one February evening that I had been through enough emotional pain and would have to pull away from being his friend as it was beginning to cause me anguish. Thomas was empathic and understanding of my request to diminish contact between us and informed me that he was unsure of his feelings towards me even though he too had begun to view our connection as more than that of simply being friends.

His wounds from his recent relationship breakup were still raw and the abrupt manner in which his then girlfriend had ended their relationship was continuing to cause him upset as he navigated his way through the terrain of grief, shock and sadness that so many of us can identify with when opening our hearts to love.

Out of respect for our connection he felt it would be unfair to turn our friendship into more and as such we tentatively agreed to remain friends; albeit from a distance for a while.

I dusted myself down in true Aries fashion; retrieving my glass and once more filling it to half full as I focused on spending time with friends and accepting invitations to go out. Thomas had been honest about his emotional state and I in turn felt a respect towards his decision to honour his feelings.

As such, February became March and just as the daffodils were blossoming I became aware that the arrival of spring had added a blossoming of Thomas's texts from chatty and practical to footloose and flirtatious. This seeming 360 degree change took me by surprise, although I would be lying if I said I wasn't thrilled, excited and curious to see what such frisky missives might become.

Thomas subsequently informed me that he and his brother were going to Egypt for a week's holiday the following week and asked whether I would like to meet up with him prior to him leaving?

I don't think fire signs are very adept at 'playing it cool' and I most certainly did my utmost to create an illusion of cool, calm and collectedness at the prospect of going over to Thomas's home. In reality I was transported back to giggling school girl emotions and giddiness. I embarked on a juice cleanse to lose those elusive Christmas pounds that were still lingering and undertook a desperate foray through the shambolic array of underwear I possessed to see if there was anything even vaguely sexy to be found!

Given that we had agreed that we would use this impromptu time together to 'talk' about where our connection may or may not go and that Thomas's spare room would be mine should we decide not to traverse from friends to benefits, I was certainly creating a commotion of preening and fussing, giggles and dieting!

It was as such that I found myself making the journey onto the M25 to Thomas's home in Kingston in early March. An uncooperative sat nav and impromptu road works did nothing to dampen the nerves that were a mixture of excitement and terror. Perhaps, just perhaps, romance wasn't quite dead.

Chapter Eight – Love Conquers All

The first hour or two were spent in friendly repartee between Thomas and I, with a little innuendo and a few flirty glances thrown into the mix. I won't deny there was a palpable sense of attraction in the air.

We had, due to the nature of a fairly long standing friendship, built a connection based on conversation, debate and a shared thirst for knowledge and understanding on myriad topics ranging from the meaning of life to dating etiquette, spiritual versus scientific, to sexual exploits!

Both having received many a battle scar from love in the past, we had intellectually explored every aspect of the merits and misgivings of entering into a physical relationship together. Such was our common love of the written word that there had even been lists compiled with 'for' and 'against' reasons for either halting or heading off into the sunset of dangerous liaison.

Needless to say that within hours of my arrival at Thomas's home, our conversation was halted in a most abrupt manner when he leant in to kiss me. Passionate connection; it was as if months of intellectually supressed notions of a relationship were cast aside with unbridled passion and urgency, as well as thoughts of preparing our meal forgotten.

We enjoyed a fantastic evening and given the fact that we shared a firm foundation of friendship and mutual trust and respect, our tentative steps into changing from friends to lovers felt natural and more powerful than two daters who had perhaps only met a few times prior.

The following day it felt strange at first as Thomas took my hand as we walked into town; so used to the walks we had previously undertaken as friends; yet it felt natural, exciting and dare I say it, meant to be.

Thomas parted for the sunnier climes of Egypt with his brother and I returned home in a haze of lust, laughter and happiness. We had regular contact during his holiday and upon his return we continued our burgeoning romance; both of us swiftly assimilating the M25 route once more.

In reality, the transition from friends to lovers in a relationship was relatively easy and natural. However, the component I hadn't factored into the mix was that for the first six months of our romance that there would be three in the relationship; albeit that the third person was oblivious to the fact.

Waking up next to Thomas to find him in tears; sobbing over his previous girlfriend was shocking. The hurt, rejection and confusion he still felt at her abrupt exit from his life the previous year was upsetting to say the least. His need for answers as to why she split from him so suddenly and without explanation, as well as the sense of loss he had attempted to bury as our union took off the ground was an unanticipated situation.

Were this any other situation with a relatively new partner, I would have taken a firm step back once the realisation hit that the person I was with was clearly not over his ex. However, given that I had been Thomas's primary source of support, solace and guidance during this time, our relationship seemed to move into a rather surreal experience whereby I would find myself being counsellor, lover and girlfriend depending on Thomas's emotional state.

Such was the strength of the bond we had shared for some years, it felt unnatural to consider walking away from the relationship at this time; yet I was most certainly confronted with my own feelings of unworthiness, not being good enough, as well as shock that our union had triggered such moments of despair and sadness within Thomas.

The part of me who had metaphorically held his hand throughout the break up with his ex understood and knew the pain he had endured and the ensuing blow it had dealt his confidence and pride. However, the part of me who had entered into a new relationship with a man I had developed a deep connection, respect and friendship for, even before the attraction had kicked in, was saddened and shocked at the level of pain and loss Thomas was displaying.

Naturally the voice of self-worth was strongly suggesting that I walk away for my own self-respect and sanity and I did feel disappointed and somewhat out of my depth in terms of how to navigate this particular relationship state of affairs I had not previously encountered!

Thomas was deeply ashamed and confused as to why our connection was triggering such depths of wounding about his ex; feelings he felt he had processed long before our relationship started. He was also apologetic and frustrated that our burgeoning connection was blighted by his ex who had callously dumped him after more than a year together, with nothing more than a phone call.

I found myself once more devaluing my own needs and feelings for the sake of someone else's as I held him as he wept and listened as he exorcised the demons of his past. I reverted back to the ever calm, nurturing and rescuing partner I had become so accustomed to being.

This one was different though, I would tell myself; this connection with Thomas was worth the upset it caused me to see him weep over his ex; he just needed more time. Now there was a line I had uttered once before I do believe!

We talked of splitting up in those early months; Thomas feeling guilty that his inability to move on from his ex was causing me upset and stress. In return I quelled the voice of self-worth; which I do believe must have sounded very jaded and battle weary by this stage in my dating journey! Thomas would on numerous occasions urge me to protect my heart; feeling that I was in a totally different emotional space to him as he was terribly confused between missing his ex and initial feelings he had for me.

A week's holiday in Morocco brought us closer in terms of being a couple and banished the third person in the relationship; albeit momentarily. In spite of an enjoyable week; my first experience of all-inclusive drinks and food, it was apparent that Thomas's emotions were complex and most certainly cerebral-based. He would, at times, appear to agonise over how he 'should' feel; mind and heart seemingly battling it out for pole position. He questioned me as to whether loving a 'regular man' would suffice for someone such as myself who had clearly sought danger and excitement in my relationship with Joe.

Again I was being reminded that while my 'story' was part of my life; a part I was determined to overcome, I had to remember that it was not part of most people's relationship repertoires! I was learning to understand the shock as well as the judgment many had on my past choices.

I would reassure Thomas that self-awareness and years of self-evaluation had afforded me a deep knowing that paths that once seemed exciting or heart-felt, no longer held any appeal or appetite for me.

I knew and indeed never doubted that Thomas was nothing but honest; baring his heart and soul was borne out of simply being someone who wore his heart on his sleeve when it came to matters of the heart. His honesty and his desire to release the shackles of the past his ex had fashioned were genuine and heartfelt and as such I respected this trait of utter honesty and transparency. However, I could not hide the fact that it hurt to hear his truths at times and to realise that he was seemingly more connected emotionally to someone no longer part of his life than he was with me. I understood his dilemma and pain but it did little to diminish my own.

Gradually, as the months progressed, even with the reality of the emotional quandaries and awareness that we were both perhaps in very different places in terms of readiness or emotional availability for a relationship, we found some kind of rhythm. Perhaps the 'scaffolding' of mutual respect, shared literary interests and an undeniable attraction, built foundations with the promise of greater construction within our relationship as time advanced.

Our rhythm consisted of each of us taking turns to drive to the other's abode, and we gradually settled into a loving relationship, with what appeared at the time to be calmer emotional waters. Indeed I was deeply touched when six months into our relationship Thomas told me he loved me; words which were mana from heaven to this sensitive soul and die hard romantic.

Honesty is such a beautiful thing isn't it; it creates open, clear communication and leaves no space for confusion or misinterpretation. I am a true proponent of the art of honesty and can, in all honesty in fact, say that Thomas was the person who has opened my eyes to the intricacies of this art form; from both a positive and negative perspective!

We would talk for hours on the phone; sometimes each night; our discussions of life, love and everything in-between did not diminish once we embarked on a physical relationship. The intellectual stimulation we enjoyed both verbally and through the written form of emails; which often became books in themselves, were on a par with the physical connection we also shared.

That said, as our relationship progressed I soon realised that Thomas was perhaps one of the most honest; I'm talking starkly so, no holds barred, verging on the soul-crushing truth that leaves nowhere to hide, kind of honest I have ever met!

The realm of email is an interesting one; enabling both sender and recipient to choose their words, their timings and responses in a manner to suit and serve their schedule. A lover of the written word as you know, I was clearly however very much a novice when it came to being the recipient of Thomas's emails. I had read about the Gemini split personality trait; the intellectual battles they endured as well as the often angst provoking indecision they experienced, but had yet to witness it first-hand.

I didn't however have to wait long until Thomas's diverse emotions appeared in my inbox. Eight months into our relationship Thomas's obvious inner emotional quandaries became more apparent. I was starkly faced with a fairly long list of his concerns, ranging from the state of my health, to the geographical distance between us, from my financial situation to our apparent lack of common interests, as well as his fear that he was not sufficiently attracted to me.

Shocking as such emails were, Thomas, in true Gemini duality, was quick to also point out his faults as he perceived them; ranging from being hot tempered and lacking in empathy, to getting bored easily and being quite needy in a relationship. His apparent necessity to identify the odds of our relationship lasting, to create certitude that love would conquer all and could be something that science, compatibility and discussion could quantify to ensure its survival, was at times exhausting, confusing and heart-breaking.

Perhaps he was right in that our seemingly opposed belief structures; mine encompassing the law of attraction and universal creation and flow, coupled with his more scientific and in his view, rational perspective, meant that ours was, as someone said to me along our journey, akin to trying to fit a square peg into a round hole?

We continued talking, loving and discussing throughout the email repartee; both of us being utterly honest. Thomas, it appeared, had vast battles within himself; stemming in part, he felt, from his fractured childhood, abandonment with his brother by both parents and subsequently being raised by strangers.

His experience of abandonment was in my view a pivotal element in his view of relationships as an adult; creating an almost unhealthy need to be needed, whilst at the same time a fear that a relationship would not last; that he would yet again be abandoned. I was fully aware and indeed deeply empathic of his understandable emotional quandaries that were at times highly challenging experiences for him; where head attempted to assimilate the words of the heart; neither able to translate the other's language.

Holidays to France and Malta ensued as did our propensity for splitting up! At first Thomas felt he needed the space to be able to see if he missed me; viewing that as an emotional signal or gauge that we could be happy together. While I would struggle with the silence, not just from my partner but also from someone who had been one of my closest friends for many years prior to entering into a relationship, I gradually became used to these moments in our on/off three year relationship that invariably saw us missing each other desperately and resurrecting communication again.

We would discuss the complexities of living closer together or indeed together, at length; from the financial implications, to the ongoing impact insomnia and times of anxiety still had on me; invariably exploring more scenarios than a movie plot! Thomas was a dedicated father to his two children and I fully respected that, as was I fully committed to ensuring that my son had as stable a home life and base as possible. Having seen him struggle through school and subsequent home education, he was finally finding his feet at college; finding his tribe of like-minded people to begin to create friendships and connections with. I was unwilling to relinquish his happiness for what would have been my selfish desire to move closer to or with Thomas.

While guilt was something I had had to work consciously and conscientiously on for many years and indeed still do at times even now, after the situation with Joe, I had assimilated many lessons and was no longer the person who let her heart lead her all those years previously. My son's wellbeing was paramount and Thomas's children were the same to him; on this aspect we were at least in total agreement.

The incredible thing was that in spite of our splits, which amounted to seven or eight in total, there remained a firm foundation of love, respect and kindness between us. There was a resonance that surpassed any tears or heartbreak Thomas and I shared together. Indeed, for two lovers of the written word, neither of us had words to describe our connection and the utter respect we felt for each other.

Perhaps we were never destined to be lovers. Perhaps our connection was one of deep love within friendship which was why we attempted, over the three year period, to make our connection fit into a love relationship; something it possibly didn't need to be.

However, our intimate relationships give us the possibility for so much growth and Thomas and I both felt that we had grown incredibly on personal and emotional levels due to our connection. I became more aware of the necessity for me to find my voice in a relationship and ditch the rescuer for good; finally honouring that love equals mutual respect, requires the ability to feel safe to be authentically you and not be belittled or judged for it. Most of all I learnt to listen; truly listen to my inner voice, intuition and heart; knowing that my inner guidance was all I really needed to move forward.

As the summer of 2017 drew to a close and the familiar chill of autumn appeared, Thomas and I had been apart for some months; both in our own ways acclimatising to being single and both dipping our toes back into the familiar dating pond again. We had remained in contact; discussing Thomas's writing and work projects and even, dare I say, Thomas becoming interested in the spiritual musings that were such a huge part of my life.

Chapter Nine – X Marks the Spot

October of 2017 saw a fellow conscious seeker connect with me through the spiritual dating site I had sheepishly joined. Such was the enormity of my belief system by this stage of my journey, on a personal and professional level, it felt vital to me that I connect with someone who walked the same path as mine in terms of fundamental beliefs. Gone was any need to debate atheism versus altruism or scientology versus spiritual healing. I knew I was ready to graduate from the school of self-worth and put my rescuer-free self into a truly balanced and equal relationship!

So, throwing my graduation hat up into the air, I was finally ready and worthy to get this relationship thing well and truly under my belt! I'd practised, experienced, laughed and cried, learnt my lessons and paid my dues; it was time for this journey to have a happy ending….surely?

Chris was kind, spiritual and a kindred soul, of that I was certain! Granted, his house located even further along the M25 could have dissuaded me, but I felt sure that by being in flow and alignment meant that I could also conquer any remaining karma the M25 needed me to release! Even a terrifying brush with death in a car accident earlier that year didn't deter me from once more departing on the now hugely familiar terrain of the M25.

He meditated; box ticked. He wasn't bad looking; another box ticked. He had a dream of setting up a spiritual retreat; big box ticked! Perhaps things were on the up, aside from the fact that the meditation soon began to take precedence over evenings out together. Invited to a friend's birthday party one Saturday night I almost began praying to the gods to break Chris's avid connection with his ancestors so that I could get my makeup on and go to the party! I was convinced that nobody used the excuse of meditation to miss a night out.

Chris then sought to heal me.

Having suffered from bouts of insomnia and anxiety due in part to my relationship with Joe, I had always been upfront with anyone I began a relationship with about my past health issues with M.E. and the impact living with Joe had had on my health. I had never relished the conversation whereby I explained what I had gone through; told partly to give the other person the choice to walk away if my past seemed too much for them to digest and partly, I always hoped, so that they would have an awareness and empathy for some of the health legacies my past still generated for me.

While at first I saw this to be a kind and considerate aspect of Chris's personality, it soon became a rather driven, dull and disappointing element that had to, apparently, be endured so that I could release the traumas of my past, learn to sleep well again and ascend to higher dimensions.

As I'm sure you can tell by now, healing the past, empowering one's health, meditation and spirituality are huge parts of my life, but it felt as if in relinquishing my own rescuer tendencies I had in fact opened the door to being rescued by another! This was most certainly a new dilemma on my quest for love.

Out of recognition that Chris had what appeared to be heart-centred intentions in wanting to heal me, I embraced as best as I could, the Shamanic chanting and the card readings, mantras and meditations. In another place and time, with a different energy and perhaps without the quite driven rescuer tendencies I was recognising in Chris, I would have possibly enjoyed and welcomed these practices as they are all elements of my own beliefs I hold dear.

Chris also sought to deter me from enjoying alcohol on an evening out or weekend together. While I respected his decision not to drink because it interfered with his connection to the spiritual realms, I was somewhat perplexed when he didn't concur with my not dissimilar reasoning for not eating meat.

It dawned on me also that while far from being an alcoholic, I enjoyed being able to share a bottle of wine with my partner or enjoy cosy nights in the pub discussing life with a gin and tonic and saw nothing wrong with that. I wasn't sure that I was ready to become teetotal or indeed willing to do so.

In fact, he became rather boring rather quickly, but I was determined not to run away immediately in typical Aries fashion. Given that Chris was also an Aries meant that I was interested to see where our somewhat tenuous connection could go, or if indeed there was anywhere for it to go to, beyond traversing the M25 that is.

Thomas and I still remained in contact and Chris was fully aware of my intermittent phone calls to my ex. During one such phone conversation however Thomas appeared out of sorts and asked if he could come to my house so that we could talk. He seemed very low when he arrived; tearful in fact and his demeanour was of concern.

It was then that Thomas informed me that he may have cancer and that he was awaiting test results.

My heart broke for this person with whom I had traversed friendship and relationship and for whom there remained a great depth of respect and care. As I hugged him I promised him I would be there as best as I could to support him through this latest part of his journey.

Honesty and authenticity being integral parts of who I had become over the years, I informed Chris of the news and said that I would, as Thomas's friend, want to support him. Chris concurred and as such we continued making tentative steps along our relationship. Thomas's subsequent diagnosis with cancer was shocking and upsetting when he called to tell me and I agreed to meet with him the following week at my home.

Through tears Thomas explained his situation from the medical and emotional choices and perspectives he was now facing and I again offered my full support through his cancer journey. However, he brought more than just his understandable pain and fear with him to my house that day, as he handed me a letter and his grandmother's ring, declaring his love for me and asking me to consider re-establishing our relationship.

Everything I had ever wanted; ring, romance and the promise of a life of love shared with my partner was being presented to me in the most inexplicable manner. I was caught up in a tidal wave of emotion, from grief and shock at Thomas's diagnosis, to incredulity at what almost amounted to a proposal, and concern at the implication such a tidal wave could have on my fledgling relationship with Chris.

Thomas informed me that he wanted me to have time to consider the situation and told me that his diagnosis had made him realise how precious life and love truly is and as such he had wanted to share his honest feelings with me regardless of whether I chose to remain with Chris or take a chance with him, or perhaps chose neither man.

Thomas departed for home and I faced a situation and decision that had appeared as a bolt out of the blue. The years spent with Thomas; fractious and unstable as they were in some ways, had been filled with happy memories, positive connection and deep love and respect. As I sat quietly pondering his words; written of course in a letter; the means through which he and I had always communicated so powerfully and poignantly, I felt lost as to which, if any decision or direction to take.

Of one thing I was certain however. Thomas's offer of commitment showed me without a shadow of a doubt that my connection with Chris, which had never truly been the meeting of spiritual souls I had hoped it would be, held nothing further for me.

It was as such that a difficult phone call ensued and our relationship ended. As Thomas and I reinstated our daily phone calls; not by design, simply out of a familiar pull perhaps, or possibly as a connection with the partial embers of love still smouldering.

Christmas of 2017 saw Thomas and I back together; not for the festive period itself as respective arrangements had already been made. Nonetheless we were reunited in heart and love was resurrected as we remained positive about his operation in January; focusing on our reignited connection and the positive possibilities it created.

Christmas came and went in a whirl of phone calls and declarations of love. Thomas and I met up for a weekend prior to his operation and it felt as if we had never been apart.

The weeks after his operation were challenging and emotional. While the operation had been a success and the prognosis appeared positive, Thomas suffered quite intensely in the aftermath, with minor complications creating physical and emotional pain for him and for those of us who cared for him.

Unable to drive, I would spend every weekend at Thomas's home; providing company, support and laughter where possible. In spite of the challenges, our love endured; weathering the storms of those dark days as January progressed. We tentatively spoke of my son and I moving to be with him in the summer once college had ended; discussing plans and possibilities as Thomas grew stronger; his body healing and emotions becoming calmer and more optimistic.

However, as he regained his strength and independence once more I began to notice the nagging doubts creeping back in to cast familiar shadows over the sunshine of our rekindled romance. Thomas's blunt retorts or insensitive remarks began to open old, sensitive wounds I had been so careful to heal since our relationship had ended previously. Mindful of my own sensitive nature and often fragile relationship with sleep, these doubts became voices I needed to listen to.

My soul; my ever patient soul began that familiar whispering to catch my attention and question my sense of self-worth once more. I began to wrestle between the ring and the romance; the connection and the promise of a life together and the whisperings once more growing louder as the recognisable feelings of unease and upset reared their heads yet again.

How do you know; *truly know* when it is time; when you know and feel it in heart and mind that you have achieved all you can achieve within a relationship? I would have thought by now that it would be a finely tuned barometer within my psyche by this stage of my relationship journeying!

In truth, I was fully aware; painfully so, that Thomas and I were simply papering over the cracks; emotionally flung together through a challenging time, yet still trying ever so hard to make the square peg fit into the round hole.

Love, respect, connection and a story traversing a little under three years had bound us together in a beautiful, blighted and deeply powerful manner as is the way of life and love for so many of us. I had by this time become acutely aware that clinging onto love as the good ship 'relation-ship' flails amongst the waves serves no purpose and simply prolongs journeys that were quite simply not meant to last a lifetime.

The lessons, respect and growth can indeed last a lifetime as is their purpose, but when we bravely accept that the journey two people share together has run its course, it is poignant, powerful and necessary to let go; release long held dreams and hopes and relinquish them to the sea of emotions that comprise so much of this human journey of self-discovery.

February 2018 saw the dual emotions of despair and hope dance together as Thomas and I parted ways; never an easy life situation to traverse, rarely with any neatly tied bows to tidy it up and smooth it over. It was as such that I stepped into a new beginning; one where I chose to embark on perhaps the most powerful relationship of my life; the one with myself.

Chapter Ten – The Gift

How refreshing to have no dating application to complete, no set of likes or dislikes to declare or need to search for the perfect profile picture. Dating myself sounded remarkably empowering and exciting in fact and something I decided to explore and experience with gusto.

There were no last minute cancellations, hastily hidden mobile phone moments or telepathic commands to any passing alien crafts to abduct a date who bore no resemblance to his profile picture!

I won't profess to waking one morning with a sudden knowing that embracing single life was the key to unlock my heart and ultimately my happiness. Rather, it was a gradual dawning of awareness and an appreciation for the growth of increased peace and balance within myself; akin to seeds, having been planted quietly in the darkness of winter, beginning to seek the light; the light of self-awareness and self-love.

It was as if, gradually, through truly appreciating the gift of learning, awareness and potential life held for me; together with acknowledging that my primary relationship is with myself and that all others are mirrors of it, that I began, moment by moment, to recognise and then embrace the fact that I needed a hiatus. It was time to truly connect with myself; without judgement, blame or recourse.

The proverbial penny had dropped and I was finally able to breathe. Within the breath came freedom; freedom to explore who I was as an individual, without the weighted labels of wife, girlfriend or date and without being at the mercy of those who wouldn't allow me the space to truly be myself.

It became an exciting and fascinating journey of self-discovery to realise that what I had been seeking was an authentic relationship where both partners see themselves as equals and are able to be their true selves within the relationship, without judgement or attachment. Recognising that each has their own journey and that they are sharing that part of the journey with each other, was actually the very opposite to what I had experienced thus far.

Each of the men I had shared portions of my life with, had been beacons to give me the opportunity to assimilate what it was that I ultimately sought from connection with another. Through experiencing what I didn't want or resonate with, I now had the opportunity to nurture and develop awareness of what true union would look and feel like to me in terms of a relationship.

The only way to truly nurture these fledgling seeds of awakening was to connect deeply with myself; diving into my feelings, needs, hopes and dreams with a sense of excitement, renewed vision and perspective. Like a child witnessing snow fall for the first time, I was in awe of the realisation I had finally given life to; viewing, being, feeling and embracing life from my empowered relationship status of being unapologetically and happily with myself!

Gratitude became and indeed remains, a huge part of my self-love process; no longer wishing my life to be perceived by myself and certainly not by others as one of 'failed relationships', 'bad choices' or 'victim-inspired representation'. Opening my eyes to the love, connection and positivity that was all around me in terms of friends, family, work projects and personal goals, it was as if those rose-tinted glasses of old had been replaced with heightened vision of the true essence of life with its infinite possibilities and incredible wisdom.

Letting go of the desperate need I had experienced in previous years, to align and measure much of my worth and identity with being in a relationship was astonishingly freeing; I felt like a born again preacher who wanted to shout this new found perception from the rooftops!

I said 'yes' to invitations, engaged more with those around me whether I was in a yoga class or out with friends; essentially I started saying 'yes' to life. I threw myself into my work, creating workshops and groups which inspired me and lit the flame of passion within me. No longer was work or evenings out with friends seen as a second rate substitute for a partner. Rather, for the first time in my life, I became fully present and engaged in the present moment; truly relishing the connections around me, as well as the bliss and empowerment of spending time alone. Like the scientist who finally completes the remaining part of a formula, so too did it feel as if I had linked all the aspects of my experiences and found the connection.

Spring turned to summer and life opened out into invitations and opportunities; saying 'yes' and engaging authentically and fully in the present moment. I was truly honouring the gifts that I realised were all around me now that I had relinquished the need for a relationship to define me or support me. I realised I was happy.

I was happy to have such freedom to make choices every day regarding all areas of my life. I was happy to build a foundation of trust and support within myself and I was happy to dye my hair whichever colour called to me without a partner suggesting an alternative would have been better!

My happiness and self-awareness, coupled with the growth the past relationships had given me reflected in my work as I began attracting clients who were experiencing their own version of relationship difficulties and dilemmas. The depth of the support I was able to share with them increased as I realised that personal experience was a powerful and valuable tool for working with others. As such, gratitude for all I had experienced grew as it touched each area of my life, embraced my emotions and being and became part of me in a profound way.

It may be hard to believe, but I had no desire to join a dating site or accept invitations from expired subscriptions to renew in order to feel complete when I discovered 'the one'. I had in fact already found 'the one' and she was quite happily enjoying the summer months, feeling free and self-contained! I hasten to add that she hadn't become a man-hater and nor was she against the idea of connecting with love when the time was right. Rather, she, albeit I will confess in the vein of true authenticity, had become slightly cynical, was pottering along doing her own thing, without the desperate, haunted look she may have possessed in previous years when she had been single for the unimaginable time of two weeks!

They say that when you stop looking for someone or cease pushing too hard to make something happen in life, you set in motion powerful forces of creation where unseen powers work behind the scenes to present you with a match to your newly held vibration. Being more in tune and in the flow of life, I was no longer attempting to micro-manage romance or diary in chapters that were not yet written.

It was in this energy that, at the very last minute, I hasten to add, I contacted a friend who was in charge of a local county fair that June, to inquire if there were any pitches remaining for myself and a fellow therapist to promote our respective businesses.

30th June 2018 was a scorching day and myself and my friend Hannah arrived in good time to set up our stall; attempting in vain to shield ourselves from the blazing hot sunshine and also appear calm and collected in true therapist fashion, whilst sweating profusely! There were pockets of brave attendees who came to peruse the various stalls as well as enjoy the welcome cool drinks and ice-creams, but many had it seems, perhaps wisely, opted to remain at home or seek solace in the shade of the garden instead.

As such the day began to drag a little as Hannah and I, boosted by a welcome Pimm's and lemonade that she had sagely suggested we required in order to see the day out, did out best to engage with the sun-burning stragglers who had bravely walked around the entire fair, including our stall which was located at the furthest most point of the field they had to traverse.

As the afternoon wore on and we became increasingly worn out, I found myself chatting with a fellow stall holder about the merits of my Quit Smoking Hypnosis sessions which she and her daughter were both interested in. Engaged in conversation I was oblivious to the fact that Hannah was enthusiastically plying one of our few 'customers' with my therapy leaflets and enthusing about the workshops I offered, having been a regular attendee herself.

Upon returning to my stall Hannah introduced Patrick to me; fellow local therapist, who, rather spookily it turned out, offered many similar therapies to myself. As previously mentioned, I felt I had accrued a fair amount of acting knowledge and experience during my childhood performances on stage; experience that stood me in good stead when confronted with deliriously dull dates. I wasn't however able to draw on my acting resources when it came to realising that, aside from the obvious connection with Patrick from a business and therapeutic stance, I found this man really quite captivating.

Attempting to the be the consummate professional, I, aided by the Pimm's, for which I shall be eternally grateful to Hannah for, managed to communicate with Patrick, holding as proficient a conversation as I could muster given the heat, alcohol and fact that he really was a very nice man, visually and conversationally.

Multi-tasking being a given for a woman, I was also able to suggest a local therapist's event I was organising as a pretext to ensure that I gave Patrick my business card, which coincidentally had my phone number on it!

As he and his four legged companion walked away from the stall after our conversation, both of us stealing another glance at the other before he and his dog rounded the corner and left my view, I turned to Hannah and in true giggling school girl fashion told her that I really hoped he would contact me and wasn't married, with someone or gay!

The heat and unexpected flurry of excitement of the afternoon wore me out and the rest of the event passed in a haze of fatigue and visions of in-depth talks with the local therapist with gorgeous blue eyes and a cheeky smile.

Considering Aries are not known for their patience, I think I did remarkably well in resisting the urge to text Patrick until later that evening. Thankfully the therapist connection gave me the perfect opportunity to contact him to say it was nice to meet him and to give him the date of the next meeting to organise the therapist's event with other local practitioners.

I waited….I would like to say patiently but I would be lying if I said that the next few days were similar to the free-flowing months prior to the county fair! Patrick did finally reply with an equally polite response, however hope turned to dismay when, for other reasons, the meeting was set back due to commitments other therapists had.

Plan B involved the all-important Facebook friending rite of passage! Vital task achieved, Patrick and I sent intermittent messages during July, but I sensed the momentum was waning and with a family holiday booked to France for the end of the month I resigned myself to the fact that perhaps I had read the signals wrong or perhaps had created signals that existed only in my head!

Bolstered by fine French wine on holiday I sent a few mildly flirtatious messages to Patrick, even suggesting we meet to discuss all matters therapeutic upon my return. He didn't dismiss the notion but wasn't, in my view, demonstrating enthusiasm for the suggestion. As it was I returned to England at the beginning of August and decided that it was time to let thoughts of a romantic connection with Patrick melt away; much like I had on that 30 degree day of June 30th!

As you can imagine therefore, it came as a huge surprise when, some weeks later Patrick called me and we enjoyed an hour long phone conversation during which we laughed, joked and generally dissected life! There followed the icing on the proverbial cake when he suggested we attend a local jazz festival one evening. Sadly rain stopped play on notions of summer jazz and the all-important Pimm's. As it transpired the next time I saw Patrick was in my lounge surrounded by six other therapists discussing the forthcoming event I was organising.

With another dose of professionalism enabling me to host the meeting whilst my heart was beating and mind wandering, the hour, after what seemed to be closer to three, signalled the end of the gathering and it was all I could do not to forcibly eject my fellow therapist friends so that Patrick and I could possibly have a conversation alone.

As I anxiously made coffee once everyone else had departed and wracked my brain for any semblance of coherent conversation, Patrick lent in and kissed me! Nerves, surprise, happiness and rather alluring thoughts intermingled as I acquiesced.

The following week saw me invite Patrick to an evening out with friends to listen to a local band. We continued our flirtation and varied conversation, oblivious to the music and company and by the end of the night I felt giddy with joy, attraction and of course Pimm's!

Our first official 'date' took place on August 17th, which happened to also be my father's birthday. Meeting Patrick from the train, we meandered along through the groups of early evening pub goers enjoying the evening sun. We enjoyed an alfresco meal as we talked and laughed; this was one date I certainly wasn't looking for an escape exit from! I can't say the same was true for Patrick though.

I had informed him that I had invited my parents for a drink at the end of the evening, given that it was my father's birthday and they had offered me a lift home. He had been happy with these arrangements until a text message from my mother asking where to meet us, lead to another cryptic message informing us that they had spotted us and would approach the table!

Patrick, glancing around for the proverbial escape route had nowhere to run, as my parents, with the stealth of marines on a secret ops mission, appeared at our table. Thankfully there was wine in copious amounts to settle Patrick's nerves at 'meeting the parents' on the very first date!

As Patrick and I waked towards the station before I departed with my parents, I, in true 'Love Island' style, forgetting my age and attempts to appear sophisticated, uttered the words every rational person over the age of 30 dreads hearing, 'Will you be my boyfriend?'! It was encouraging to see that throughout my dating and relationship journey I had not lost that confident Aries streak, or naivety as some might call it, to shove allure and mystique aside in favour of bounding straight in there without a shred of subtlety!

There is an important 'aside' I would like to mention at this point in the story. Many years previously, soon after my marriage to Joe had ended, a good friend and psychic had told me that there was a man waiting for me who wore a suit and that he would rekindle my faith in men and relationships. She even went so far as to call him the 'Gentleman in the Suit.'

Over the ensuing years when none of my dates resembled this suited gentleman I would quiz Lesley occasionally or joke about yet another date who wasn't the suited gentleman and she would tell me he was still there, waiting to enter my life at the right time. Subsequently she told me he had hung up his suit and was now appearing to her wearing shorts; suggesting a change of career or life path. Still I waited.

The mystery was finally solved when it transpired that Patrick had worked for some years as the 'Pinstriped Medium' and had pictures of himself wearing a suit when he did readings or psychic work. He'd subsequently stopped focusing on both his mediumship and city work to re-train as a therapist; hence the change of clothing he appeared to Lesley in. Not that I am suggesting that we therapists only wear shorts you do understand!

My suited gentleman took his time to enter my life and even took his time showing interest in me once he had, but there's no doubting that he was presented to me many moons ago when life, love and relationships were at their lowest ebb.

As my story draws to a close for now, I look back at that tapestry that at times seemed laden with fear, pain and desperation and at others with humour, growth and acceptance and can see the perfect tableau my journey thus far has created. Patrick and I celebrated a year's connection on June 30th 2019 by revisiting the same county fair where destiny and faith brought us together; both of us having reached out across the waves of energy that permeate every aspect of our lives, to continue the relationship expedition together.

Patrick and I have at this point in our respective journeys come together as a meeting of equals. There have been the usual hurdles to overcome and differences to assimilate that any couple experiences, but the basis of transformation with this relationship which sets it aside from those previously, is that I have consciously put the learning and growth generated from previous connections into practice.

Therein also lies the gift. I don't always get it right and nor would I hope to. We are growing and evolving all the time and it is through the ups and downs of a relationship, if there is trust and mutual respect at the fore, that we truly unite; honouring our individual paths but choosing to share them, with open and honest communication, humour and a deep care for the growth, wellbeing and life of the other.

Typing this final paragraph on a cold January day of 2020 I know that my journey to the heart continues and that the growth, awareness and connection I have made within myself is the precious gift I have allowed myself to receive. Patrick and I are looking forward to revisiting the county fair this year and he knows that mine is a large Pimm's!

P.S.

Re-editing my story for the umpteenth time in July 2020 it feels fitting to add a little P.S. Life for us all has changed in ways we could not have foreseen as we heralded in the new year this January.

Needless to say, Patrick and I didn't get to the county fair this year. We, like so many have ridden the waves of the choppy seas of uncertainty, and indeed, still are. I won't pretend this has been easy because it has required all of us to make vast adjustments in our lives.

We have however acclimatised to enjoying a more simplistic life; finding gratitude in things that were perhaps previously taken for granted. I can however assure you that Patrick's supply of Pimm's has been appreciated and enjoyed during the early summer months thus far! We've even branched out to cocktails on occasion!

Lessons Learned and Wisdom Gained

* **We cannot truly love someone else fully if we do not love ourselves.**

You are ultimately your one true love; the one you share the highs and lows of your life with. If you cannot value, respect and nurture your relationship with yourself, how can you seek to share love with another? All true love starts from within and radiates outwards connecting with the other people we journey through life with.

* **We accept the love we feel we deserve.**

If we do not take the time to check in with and understand our version of love and relationship and get to know our own values, boundaries and needs, we are not ready to open our heart to another. Love does not disrespect or lie and ultimately we deserve the kind of love that is built on honesty, respect and trust. The right person is someone who knows your worth and has your best interests at the core of their heart.

* **Love is a choice.**

Love is ultimately a choice; a decision we take once a relationship has traversed the initial moments of infatuation or rose-tinted glasses. It is a choice to be with someone in spite of their flaws and to love them for their flaws anyway. We are all works in progress and a truly kindred spirit is someone who embraces you; all of you, including the rough edges and tears, the imperfections and the disagreements.

* Love does not seek to change you.

We don't ever have to change to make someone love us. We only change because we choose to do so for ourselves. Changing in order to keep someone with you can never result in happiness. True love is appreciating the qualities and the flaws and trusting that the right person will see us as perfect just the way we are; knowing we are imperfect but loving us regardless. None of us is 'perfect'; we are not meant to be, so don't change to make love stay.

* Love can never be forced.

We can't make someone love us, no matter how much we may think the union would be perfect. Love is a two way street and there has to be a meeting mid-way of emotion, commitment, values and respect. If someone pulls away from you and you seek even harder to win them back, you will probably push them further away. You lose yourself in trying to get them to love you back. You deserve greater love than that, so don't settle for less.

* Don't lose yourself in love.

Being in love is wonderful, as is sharing life's journey with another. However, love doesn't mean giving up your friends or hobbies and interests and losing sight of your own personal goals and visions. True love enables two people to share their journey whilst honouring their own separate path at the same time. Co-dependence is not healthy for either person, so enjoy your shared experiences, but equally, value and encourage your own and never lose sight of your relationship with YOU.

Contact

If you would like to connect with me personally or find out more about my work as a transformational therapist, please follow one of the links below:

www.pathwaytherapies.co.uk

www.facebook.com/stepontoyourpath

katja@pathwaytherapies.co.uk

If you would like to join my tribe of writing supporters and connections, please join the group at:

www.facebook.com/lovearoundthem25

I look forward to connecting with you.

With love, gratitude and laughter as you journey along your relationship and life pathway.

Your fellow adventuring soul, Katja x

Printed in Great Britain
by Amazon